st. john's wort

st. john's wort

THE MOOD ENHANCING HERB

Christopher Hobbs, L.AC.

St. John's Wort: The Mood Enhancing Herb
Christopher Hobbs

Cover design: Bren Frisch
Illustrations: Susan Strawn Bailey
Book design: Dean Howes

Text copyright 1997, Christopher Hobbs

Botanica Press is an imprint of Interweave Press

 Interweave Press, Inc.
201 East Fourth Street
Loveland, Colorado 80537-5655
USA

Printed in the United States of America

Library of Congress Cataloging-in-Publication Data

Hobbs, Christopher, 1944–
      St. John's wort: the mood enhancing herb / by Christopher
Hobbs
            p.   cm.
      Includes bibliographical references and index
      ISBN 1-883010-45-4

First printing: 10M:897:PP
Second printing: 7.5M:598:UG

Acknowledgments

A special thanks to Beth Baugh for help with every aspect of this project, from research and editing to personal encouragement. My gratitude also to the German researchers, scientists, and practitioners who lighted the path to greater knowledge about St. John's wort.

Doree Pitkin provided her excellent editorial skills, and to all the people at Interweave Press who made this book a reality, my special appreciation.

CONTENTS

INTRODUCTION

❧

ONE OF THE most excit-
ing herbs today is St.
John's wort, a weedy little
plant with a yellow bloom
that has been an esteemed
part of herbal medicine for
centuries. Not only does
this plant grow willingly
and widely, it has a track
record of effectiveness and
safety for treating depression and its accompanying
symptoms, anxiety and in-
somnia. Certain kinds of injuries also respond to treatment with St. John's wort.
Although many herbalists
and traditional healers have
used this herb successfully,
only recently have scientific
studies confirmed the effectiveness and safety of St.
John's wort.

WHAT TO EXPECT FROM THIS BOOK

This book offers insights
into depression, anxiety,

and insomnia as well as specific and practical information about using St. John's
wort, a safe and effective
natural medicine. You'll dis-
cover how to choose a good
commercial product and
how to make your own
preparations of St. John's
wort. Other calming, and
sleep-promoting herbs are
included, too. In a concise
and readable format, learn
about:

• Why scientific researchers
  are excited about St.
  John's wort

• How to ease depression,
  anxiety, and insomnia naturally

• How to use St. John's
  wort to treat

  • Wounds

  • Burns and other injuries

- Ulcers

- Nerve damage and more

- A complete review of St. John's wort's history of use, chemistry, pharmacology, and toxicology

- A review of what a doctor will do about depression, anxiety, and insomnia.

Many people have questions about St. John's wort. Here are some of the most commonly asked, along with the answers:

Q. *What is St. John's wort good for?*

A. When taken properly, this herb has helped many to overcome depression and related problems. It also helps heal wounds and burns.

Q. *Is it safe?*

A. In both scientific studies and traditional practice,

very few who have taken St. John's wort report side effects; an increased sensitivity to light is the most common. Compared to the varied and sometimes dangerous side effects of pharmaceutical antidepressants, St. John's wort is extremely safe.

Q. *If St. John's wort is safe and effective, why haven't we known about it for a long time? Why are we hearing about it just now?*

A. Herbalists have known about this herb for centuries. Two thousand years ago, physicians mentioned St. John's wort as a healing plant. A thousand years ago, in the Middle Ages, St. John's wort was cited as a protection against possession by spirits and demons and the effects of witches' spells, conditions we would define today as mental disorders.

Early in this century, a German physician who was familiar with traditional herbalism began to study St. John's wort. In 1935 he began a twelve-year study of the herb and its uses, arousing interest in the medical and scientific community. Since then, we've learned a lot more about St. John's wort, and we also know much more about the brain and mood disorders, too, making this compre-hensive information available to us for the first time.

The book you are about to read contains a concise and carefully researched summary of current knowledge about St. John's wort. It also includes information about other herbs and dietary measures to help support the nervous system and the entire body in its efforts to maintain excellence in both physical and emotional health.

St. John's Wort

CHAPTER 1

ST. JOHN'S WORT AND HOW TO USE IT

❧

C LINICAL DEPRESSION affects over fifteen percent of the population. In the United States, this means that over 40 million people will experience clinical depression and associated symptoms such as anxiety and insomnia. To get through the day and survive the night, millions count on pharmaceutical drugs to change brain chemistry and even alter personality.

Paxil, Prozac, the tricyclic antidepressants, and other drugs are new; the oldest, the tricyclics, date only from the 1950s, and their long-term effects are still unknown even to psychiatrists and research scientists. Will continued use of these drugs overstimu-late or otherwise damage the nervous system, leaving it devastated after ten or twenty years? Do they have subtle but cumulative effects on such internal organs as the liver, effects that appear only after decades of use? Or are these drugs truly the panaceas that many take them to be?

We don't know the answers to these questions yet, but we do know that St. John's wort, a common weed in many countries, reduces and even eliminates symptoms of depression. Scientific researchers in this century, taking a cue from traditional medicine, have subjected the herb to rigorous study and confirmed its effectiveness and safety.

We also know that many mood disorders respond to healthy habits such as exercise, exposure to natural light during a walk, good diet, and regular dietary supplements of herbs and phytonutrients. Traditional healers excel in using these tools; they treat ailments with a view to the health of the whole person, not just the person's parts.

Some doctors in the United States and Europe are routinely recommending, and even prescribing, St. John's wort to patients suffering from depression. In Europe, the herb has been prescribed by physicians for mood disorders for over sixty years. In the United States, the herb is increasingly being tried. It has been featured in major newspaper and magazine articles and on television shows, and even conservative doctors are fervently expressing the hope that the herb will be "the next Prozac, with fewer side effects".

Is St. John's Wort Right for You?

Answering this question requires you to carefully consider your own condition, and perhaps ask for help in doing so. In some situations it is advisable to see a holistically oriented physician with some experience with St. John's wort, a qualified Western herbalist (phytotherapist), an herbalist trained in Traditional Chinese Medicine, or a naturopathic doctor. These traditional practitioners are qualified to conduct complete examinations, to make diagnoses, and to design a total-health program that fits your specific situation. Visit one of these practitioners before beginning to use St. John's wort if any of the following apply to you:

• You have been diagnosed as having major depression, bipolar illness (formerly manic depression), or another mood or personality disorder

- You are taking prescribed medications such as Prozac, Paxil, or Zoloft; tricyclic antidepressants such as amitriptyline, nortriptyline, imipramine, or desipramine; benzodiazepines such as Valium and Xanax; or any other mood- or neurotransmitter-altering substances

- You are drinking alcoholic beverages or taking recreational drugs. Such substances are a poor choice for those struggling with depression, for they disturb brain chemicals and processes that are already disrupted by the illness.

When to Try St. John's Wort

It makes a lot of sense to try the natural way of healing before plunging into the risky world of pharmaceutical drugs whose unknown side effects can sometimes mask symptoms of illness. Taken as part of a complete program that includes a healthy diet, proper exercise, counseling, and herbal remedies, St. John's wort is a logical first step toward effectively and safely relieving symptoms of depression, anxiety, and insomnia, as well as ultimately achieving a higher level of health.

St. John's wort may ease insomnia by increasing nighttime levels of melatonin in blood plasma, thus encouraging sleep. When thirteen healthy volunteers took a preparation of the herb containing 0.53 milligrams of total hypericin for three weeks, their nocturnal levels of melatonin increased (Demisch et al 1991).

Major depression and bipolar disorder are serious illnesses that require the care of a qualified medical practitioner. Yet depression and bipolar disorder often occur in mild to moderate

PROZAC FOR KIDS?

Last year, nearly 600,000 children and adolescents took Prozac, Paxil, or Zoloft, although these drugs are not approved for use by children. Recently Eli Lilly, the makers of Prozac, submitted a mountain of documents to the United States Food and Drug Administration (FDA) in hopes of achieving official approval for prescribing these powerful medications to children. Even pets are taking Prozac; dogs with difficult personality problems seem to be calmed by the drug.

Some young people have been taking Prozac for up to ten years. A Long Island girl began when she was 5 years old because strangers terrified her. Counseling failed, but Prozac apparently has been successful, for the girl is now in her school's honors program.

Not all researchers are convinced that giving Prozac and similar drugs to children is a good thing, however. Dr. Leon Eisenberg, professor of social medicine at Harvard Medical School, recently noted that "even a good drug can be abused; look what happened with Ritalin. The availability of the pill has allowed doctors to disregard the importance of trying to find out what's going on with these kids."

What if teenagers are medicated just for being teenagers? Marsha Levy Warren, a Manhattan clinical psychologist, was recently quoted in *The New York Times* (Sunday, Aug. 10, 1997): "If we are giving them medication to stabilize their moods, they may not be able to handle the ebb and flow of emotion that is part of life." The book *It's Nobody's Fault* (Koplewicz 1996) discusses this issue more extensively. For children and young people who are truly suffering from depression, perhaps a gentler yet effective solution would be St. John's wort.

cases that are troublesome but do not disrupt one's life or destroy the ability to function normally. In such cases, the use of St. John's wort may be of great benefit. If you are unsure about evaluating the kind of depression that concerns you, work with your health practitioner to diagnose or rule out the presence of major depression.

The following situations frequently respond very well to the use of St. John's wort:

• Recurring mild to moderate depression that persists for days, weeks, or months

• Mood swings that alternate between mild to moderate depression and elation or excitability, or mild to moderate depression and irritability or restlessness

• Mild anxiety, especially when coupled with feeling down or depressed

• Mild anorexia (loss of appetite) associated with mood swings

• Insomnia when coupled with mood swings involving depression.

Other Effective Uses

Although St. John's wort has been highlighted as a useful treatment for depression, it offers other significant benefits as well. Many of these uses coincide with ancient reports that the herb helps those with mental disorders; in fact, a very early text encourages the use of St. John's wort as a healing balm for burns and a protection against "mania".

St. John's wort helps heal and ease the pain of wounded nerves. Neuralgia, or nerve pain, ranges from a severe, stabbing pain to a dull, chronic pain caused by injuries and various nervous-system disorders. St. John's wort is often beneficial in treating this pain. Even nerves that have been cut, such as in surgery, can respond to St. John's wort used both internally and externally.

Sciatica, a nerve inflammation that causes pain to shoot down the leg due to spinal-disk damage, often improves with the application of St. John's wort oil or tincture two or three times a day. However, the use of preparations of St. John's wort for peripheral neuralgia must be coupled with a complete diagnosis and workup from a qualified health practitioner or physician.

ST. JOHN'S WORT FOR PAIN AND INJURIES

St. John's wort is renowned as a dependable wound-healing herb to ease the pain and inflammation for all kinds of external skin trauma including burns, cuts, and abrasions, as well as muscular and nerve injuries such as strains, sprains and pinched nerves.

Modern research is just now revealing the herb's action on the molecular and cellular levels. Researchers have found that extracts of St. John's wort can both suppress the immune response to lower excessive inflammation, reducing pain and swelling, and enhance other aspects of our immune processes, perhaps helping to enhance the healing process. For instance, the tannin or polyphenol fraction can stimulate the mononuclear phagocyte system, which are immune cells that remove waste products from our blood and tissues. The fat-soluble compounds can reduce other aspects of immunity (Evstifeeva & Sibiriak, 1996).

St. John's wort is also a powerful antioxidant, more potent than many other well-known tonic and protecting herbs such as eleuthero, schisandra, or ginseng (Bol'shakova et al, 1997). It is not known whether this effect plays a role in the antidepressive activity of St. John's wort, but it is probably significant in the herb's ability to lower inflammation and pain in burns and injuries.

Preparations for Healing Wounds

Oil of St. John's wort is applied directly to wounds and burns to ease pain and encourage healing. These preparations are made by grinding the flowering tops of the plant and soaking them in vegetable oil. Like tincture, a good oil should be bright red to red orange. The most potent products are those that are home-made, although commercial products from reliable companies are also effective.

The desired ingredient for treating wounds and burns is not hypericin, but the antibacterial hyperforin. This ingredient is fairly stable when stored out of the light in a dark, sealed bottle with little air space inside; it

remains effective for three months when correctly stored. Refrigeration slows the breakdown of the effective ingredients. About five months of storage is the maximum, however, so it is a good idea to look for products stamped with the date of manufacture or an expiration date, and to date the products you make yourself.

St. John's wort is useful in treating the following injuries:

• Abrasions. When immediately applied, St. John's wort rarely fails to ease the pain of a scrape or abrasion, such as a skinned knee. It also relieves the pain caused by blows such as hitting your thumb with a hammer or dropping something heavy on your toe.

• Burns. To treat serious second-degree burns and any third-degree burns, see a physician immediately. For first-degree burns and mild to moderate second-degree burns, apply St. John's wort oil, cream, or salve to the affected area. The herb speeds the healing of first- and second-degree burns and can help reduce their pain. For use on burns, St. John's wort preparations are often mixed with other specific herbs that benefit the skin, such as plantain and calendula.

• Ligament, tendon, and muscle strains or sprains result in inflammation and pain. St. John's wort helps treat these injuries, but its effectiveness is enhanced when arnica oil or tincture is added. However, do not use arnica preparations on broken skin.

The following uses of St. John's wort are also usually safe and effective:

• For bedwetting and night-terrors in children,

use half the normal adult dose or less of tincture, depending on the age and size of the child

• Mood swings associated with menopause or premenstrual syndrome

• In some cases of epilepsy, the herb is helpful when taken internally

• St. John's wort oil is sometimes taken by mouth to ease the symptoms of ulcers.

• One teaspoon of St. John's wort oil, injected into and retained in the lower bowel overnight, helps the pain of irritable bowel syndrome and piles.

St. John's Wort and AIDS

About ten years ago, researchers found that St. John's wort has a strong antiviral effect.

While most of the international interest in St.

John's wort centers on its antidepressive and mood-enhancing effects, a number of clinical studies show that it has great promise as a broad-spectrum antiviral for patients with AIDS, or those who are HIV positive. The powerful effect of St. John's wort on the AIDS virus was discovered in 1988. The first international patents had been taken out in 1986 on hypericin and pseudohypericin for their inhibitory effects against a variety of viruses, including influenza and herpes simplex types I and II. A year later, the researchers reported on St. John's wort's action against retroviruses, such as the HIV virus. The antiviral effect was found to be unlike those of some of the other pharmaceutical antivirals such as Acyclovir and AZT (Meurelo et al 1988). In 1992, ongoing clinical trials were being developed and are now under way (Gulick et al 1992).

The herb extract, standardized to hypericin, and the purified hypericin itself seem to provide AIDS patients with a better quality of life by helping to lift the depression and anxiety associated with a life-threatening illness.

Some studies indicate that the herb significantly lowers the amount of virus in the body. It may also improve patients' immune status by increasing T-helper cells. The major side effect of St. John's wort, that of increasing one's sensitivity to light (photosensitization), may be important to its antiviral activity. Light exposure may increase its antiviral effects and may be essential to the action.

Currently, a number of clinical trials involving AIDS patients are proceeding in the United States, Israel, and elsewhere to determine the effectiveness, proper dose, and scope of activity of St. John's wort. This herb may well prove

THE PROS AND CONS OF STANDARDIZATION

When an herbal extract is examined by modern scientific methods such as high-performance liquid chromatography (HPLC) or gas chromatography/mass-spectroscopy, it is possible to detect chemical compounds in the plant. Many have been identified from St. John's wort, and you can review these in the literature review under the chemistry section in the back of this book. For years, it was thought that most of the activity of St. John's wort was due to the red coloring pigment of the plant, called hypericin, or "hypericum red." While this compound has definite therapeutic activity, such as an antiviral effect, it is now known that the whole plant with all its numerous compounds in their natural balance works best for depression and probably for other uses of St. John's wort as well.

Several years ago, companies began selling St. John's wort products standardized to a higher percentage of hypericin. These products resulted from using industrial solvents to selectively extract and purify the compound from large quantities of the herb. In this process, other compounds not considered necessary for the overall activity of St. John's wort were eliminated. This process is also commonly used with other medicinal plants such as milk thistle, ginkgo, and ginseng.

The German researchers who developed many of these modern "phytopharmaceuticals" recently reversed their thinking on standardization. Max Wichtl, a leading German researcher, said, during the keynote address of a major medicinal plant conference in London in June, 1996, "Don't equate efficacy with standardization." This means that most effective preparations contain many active compounds, not just one. The quality of any preparation also depends on the freshness and quality of the original herb used in the product, and how the herb was dried and extracted.

Today, most tablet and capsule products of St. John's wort

contain a powdered extract with a guaranteed level of 0.3 percent hypericin, because this is about the highest level that the plant can contain in its natural state. Nearly all companies sell identical extract, manufactured by the same supplier, although labels and prices vary from company to company.

In these products, hypericin is used simply as a "marker" to ensure that the product contains St. John's wort flowers. This practice is sound because the active constituents correlate closely to hypericin. Remember that most of the standardized St. John's wort tablet and capsule products are mass-produced. That is why they generally cost about one-third less than the high-quality, hand-made tinctures from highly reputable companies in the United States and Europe. With tinctures, quality assurance can be performed by anyone who uses the product. Simply check the color and taste.

to be a vital tool in overcoming this twentieth-century plague.

NATURAL MEDICINE

According to ancient traditional systems of healing such as Traditional Chinese Medicine, one's fundamental constitutional type influences reactions to the world. This genetic makeup, or "hardwiring," is largely determined by the gifts received from ancestors, but it can be strongly influenced and even changed. Any trait can be modified and prevented from becoming a lasting negative influence on health, happiness, and effectiveness. For instance, one who has a "novelty gene" that predisposes him to a strong desire for constant exposure to new experiences, people, situations, and ideas may have difficulty making commitments, staying in one place, or focusing on anything for very long. Perhaps this gift for inquisitiveness can become an advantage, opening avenues to becoming a scientist or investigative reporter who travels, explores, and writes about the world, thus touching the lives of others in a positive way.

Treating the Root, Treating the Branch

Natural medicine includes the concept of treating the root or treating the branch. Think of the body as a tree that takes root. Treating the branch means to treat unwanted symptoms, while treating the root means seeking to understand one's nature and using diet, herbs, exercise, and other means to bring about harmony and balance with oneself, with family and friends, and within the environment. Modern medicine often seeks to treat the branch by using pharmaceutical drugs that shock the body into a different symptom-complex or mask

symptoms, without really addressing the more difficult (and less profitable) issues of health.

Practitioners of natural medicine seek to understand the deeper issues and work on them. Symptoms are addressed in order to ease pain and suffering and increase energy, but these practitioners believe that this is only a part of the complete picture. Though treating the branch is often necessary, it is only by treating the root that lasting health can be achieved.

Choosing a Good Product

Once you have determined that St. John's wort is safe for your condition, choose an effective product. Several brands of St. John's wort products are available in natural products stores, herb shops, pharmacies, discount stores, and even supermarkets. I suggest you purchase the product in your local natural products store or herb shop, because the staff is likely to have significantly more training and knowledge about the products than staff at other establishments. Personnel at the specialty stores, particularly if they have worked in the field for a few years or more, are usually well-prepared to answer questions about specific products and help you compare their quality, potency, and dosage. If you are confused about what product to buy, be assured that nearly every product from a reputable manufacturer is more or less effective. For a more certain recommendation, consult an herbalist or natural-health practitioner. Many reputable St. John's wort products are standardized to 0.3 percent hypericin, the constituent that contains the red pigment characteristic of preparations of St. John's wort.

You are likely to find two basic preparations of St. John's wort: liquid, alcohol-

MAKING A ST. JOHN'S WORT JUICE POWDER AT HOME

To make a dried juice powder, process the fresh herb by juicing it in a juicer or mill. Return the pulp to the juice and stir well. Spread the pulp onto the fruit-leather trays of a food dehydrator or pour into Pyrex baking dishes and dry in the oven at the lowest heat, with the door propped slightly open. Once the product is thoroughly dry, powder it in a blender or coffee grinder and store in a tightly sealed glass jar.

This dried juice powder should be between 0.1 and 0.3 percent total hypericin. You'll find that it is an excellent and potent product. Put the powder into 00-size capsules and take one capsule twice daily.

based tinctures in one- or two-ounce amber bottles with droppers, and capsules or tablets containing powdered extracts. I prefer tinctures because they are absorbed efficiently and quickly by the body. They're also easy to take, particularly for people who have difficulty swallowing tablets and capsules.

Try to find tinctures with an extraction ratio of 1:2 or 1:3; these are more potent than products with a 1:5 or higher extraction ratio, although less common. Hold a dropperful of tincture up to the light and evaluate its color; a good tincture from a reputable company should be a dark, rich red or dark red-brown and often nearly fluorescent. If it is clear to pink, the tincture will not be effective. The taste of the tincture should be slightly astringent and resinous, with very little bitterness. Avoid glycerites of St. John's wort because they are weaker than tinctures.

Some people, especially those who don't like alcohol, prefer capsules or tablets. These products typically contain extract powders that are made by soaking the flowering tops of St. John's wort in methanol (wood alcohol), spraying the liquid onto a carrier such as lactose, and then evaporating the alcohol until only minute trace amounts are left. Powders used in capsules and tablets are harder to evaluate by color and taste because the carriers used to adjust the potency of the finished extract often change its flavor and color.

Some tablets and capsules contain powdered extracts made with industrial solvents such as hexane and acetone. Although these substances are completely removed from the finished extracts, I recommend avoiding such products. Call the manufacturer of the product if you are unsure what solvents are used in the manufacturing process.

STEP BY STEP: MAKING ST. JOHN'S WORT PREPARATIONS AT HOME

Growing St. John's wort in your garden, getting to know it, and making your own preparations are very satisfying activities. Herbalism is the medicine of the people, and it has been so for thousands of years. Much of the healing power of plants can develop from the process of growing, touching, and smelling them, and using them for your own preparations.

If you would like to make St. John's wort preparations at home, follow these easy steps to produce tincture, dried juice powder, oil, and salve. Because this herb grows so abundantly, you may find some growing near your home, or you may wish to grow it yourself. Otherwise, seek the dried herb at your local herb shop or request it from sources listed in the Resource Directory in the back of this book.

If you grow or find St. John's wort, harvest the top Five to seven inches when the plant is flowering, usually in June or early July. Most of the flowers should be in the bud stage, with only a few fruit capsules developing.

Each type of St. John's wort product requires that the plants first be crushed or ground before use. I like to rinse the fresh, flowering tops to remove any dust, then run them through a wheat-grass juicer or Corona grain mill to produce a beautiful, bright-red, juicy pulp.

Tincture. The best alcohol for making tinctures is 190-proof grain alcohol. If you cannot obtain this locally, see the Resource Directory for companies that will ship it to your door. To make a small amount of tincture for personal use, 100-proof vodka will work,

27

but the product is weaker; you should take up to twice the dose recommended for commercial tincture.

To prepare a tincture, fill a clean, clear glass jar about half full of alcohol. Put in as much pulp and juice as possible. The pulp will settle; if it rises above the level of the liquid after settling, add alcohol to completely cover the pulp. If the pulp is not covered by liquid, the solution can ferment and taste bad.

If you are using dried flowering tops, put the herb and alcohol into a blender and blend to make a smooth liquid. Don't use so much herb that the brewing tincture is too dry; after the pulp settles, you should see about half an inch of clear red liquid above the herb.

Cover the jar tightly and shake it daily for two weeks. Then filter the liquid out of the pulp using a linen cloth or filtering paper and squeezing out the last drops. Discard the pulp. The liquid should be bright red and can be bottled and used immediately. Store it in a cool place away from direct light and heat. One-half to one teaspoon morning and evening is the proper dose. Children and the elderly can benefit from a smaller amount.

If you are using dried herb for the tincture, you may have to put your jar in direct sunlight for a day or two at the end of the two weeks of soaking time in order to develop the desired red color. If the tincture remains pale, the herb was probably too old and your product is weak. Find a better quality dried herb, perhaps by consulting the Resource Directory for suppliers; use the weak tincture to extract the new batch of herb.

Oils and Salves. Both oils and salves from fresh or dried St. John's wort begin with the pulp that has been ground or juiced. The oil must be made first, for it is a component of the salve; of course, the oil alone can be rubbed into the skin.

Prepare a clean, clear glass jar and fill it half full of extra-virgin olive oil or another light vegetable oil of your preference. Add St. John's wort juice and pulp and let the pulp settle. Good quality dried herb, blended at high speed in the oil, can also work. If the pulp is above the surface of the oil, add more oil. The pulp must be completely covered by the oil at all times; if not, fermentation can begin.

Check the jar daily and add oil if needed. Shake the bottle vigorously every day for two weeks. Then use linen or filter paper to separate the pulp and the red oil, squeezing the last bits of oil from the pulp by hand. You may have to place the jar in the sunlight for two days or so to help

the oil develop a red color. If the oil is not red, or at least a rich, dark color, find a better-quality herb. Use the pale oil to soak another batch of herbs until you do get a good, red color and a potent product.

To make salve, grate beeswax into St. John's wort oil that has been warmed in a saucepan on the stove, stirring frequently. Test the consistency of the salve by cooling the underside of a spoonful of the salve in ice water until the salve firms up. The salve should be semi-hard but spread easily onto the skin. Add more beeswax if it is too soft; add more oil if it is too hard. Pour the finished salve into small half-ounce jars or other suitable containers to harden.

Proper Dose

For the average person weighing 140 pounds, use these guidelines unless advised otherwise by your health-care practitioner.

Adjust the dose according to your weight, age, and state of health. Weak people, very thin people, people with compromised liver function, children, and the elderly should take less. The advice of a health-care practitioner is also necessary when contemplating long-term use or facing severe symptoms or illness.

When using St. John's wort for depression, the recommended dose of tincture or liquid extract is two droppersful (2 milliliters), twice daily. The range of dose recommended by experienced herbalists varies from about thirty drops (slightly less than one dropperful) to three droppersful, three times daily. To determine the level of total hypericins in a well-made tincture, we sent a sample to a laboratory to be tested by ultraviolet absorption, high-performance liquid chromatography (HPLC). The test revealed that the tincture contained about 0.05 percent hypericins. This means that every milliliter of tincture will contain 0.37 milligrams of hypericins. One milliliter equals approximately one dropperful, or thirty-five drops of liquid.

Dosage of Liquid Tincture

Initial Dose: Begin with a dose of two droppersful twice daily. Increase to a double dose if desired effects are not felt after four to six weeks. Not all tinctures are as strong as the one we tested.

Full dose: One-half to one teaspoon (three to five droppersful) of dark-red tincture, morning and evening; or one to two droppersful of the tincture, three times daily between mealtimes.
Cost: $25 to $34 per month

Dosage of Capsules

For capsules standardized to 0.3 percent hypericin,

take one 300-milligram capsule two or three times daily before meals. If you don't get the results you are looking for, you can safely go up to two capsules, three times daily. It is best to start with the lower dose first. Capsule dosages also apply to tablets.

Cost: $18 to $27 per month

For comparison, a prescription of Paxil costs approximately $65 per month.

Dosage of Tea Infusion

To make a tea infusion, select dried herb that contains some yellow flowers. For each cup of tea, simmer one to two teaspoons of the cut and sifted herb in a cup of water for five minutes. Remove from heat and let steep for twenty minutes, then strain and drink one or two cups each morning before eating and one cup at night, preferably after the evening meal.

Using St. John's Wort Oil

Oil of St. John's wort, should be dark red. Take one teaspoon on an empty stomach, morning and evening. The oil can be combined with a soothing tea, such as marshmallow root (one part), licorice (1/4 part), and peppermint (1/2 part), taken two or three times daily, also on an empty stomach.

How Fast Does St. John's Wort Work?

The 1996 monograph on St. John's wort by the European Scientific Cooperative for Phytomedicines (ESCOP) states that "an antidepressant effect is not expected before ten to fourteen days of treatment." Rudolph Weiss, M.D. and renowned herbalist, states in his book *Herbal Medicine* that "the mood lightening effect does not develop quickly—it is necessary to give the drug not just four weeks, but probably two or three months. The first effects will usually be noted after two or three weeks."

In reviewing twenty-five controlled clinical trials with St. John's wort for depression, and the progression of its clinical effects, two German researchers report that "as with the synthetic antidepressants, a treatment period of four weeks appears to be necessary and adequate for evaluating the effectiveness of St. John's wort preparations."

My clinical experience shows that these researchers are right. If a patient hasn't seen any effects from St. John's wort after four weeks of taking it for depression, the herb is unlikely to be effective for that person, and re-evaluation is required. Some may decide to give the herb another four weeks to make sure, and I have seen some people begin to respond after six weeks.

It is more likely that the patient will feel some effect after two or four weeks, but the full effects may not de-velop for two to three months. If no effects are felt after three months, it is advisable to discontinue the St. John's wort preparation. As with any medication, herbal or pharmaceutical, the long-term safety of St. John's wort for any particular individual is impossible to predict.

Externally, St. John's wort oil or tincture, applied to help relieve the pain of scrapes, burns, and cuts, works within minutes. In fact, these products are some of the fastest and most effective pain relievers for external skin trauma. For deeper pain like neuropathy (nerve inflammation and pain), St. John's wort oil might take several days to work well, or even as much as a week; the oil and its active constituents must penetrate the skin. The immune-altering and anti-inflammatory effects of the oil will help relieve these kinds of deeper pain.

Step by Step: Replacing Antidepressants with St. John's Wort

Some patients who take antidepressants experience difficulty in discontinuing the drugs. St. John's wort and other herbs can be used to support the process of discontinuation, but it is essential to work with a health-care practitioner or doctor trained in herbal medicine when attempting to replace psychoactive pharmaceuticals. I have found that it is best to take from three to six months to make this transition, and that many benefit from following a three-step program.

Step 1. Begin by establishing a total program for health with an experienced herbalist, practitioner of Traditional Chinese Medicine, naturopathic doctor, or other qualified health-care practitioner. The program should include stress release, self-massage, receiving bodywork, and an herbal program to eliminate deficiencies such as adrenal weakness. Healthy diet, conscious breathing, meditation, visualization, and a progressive exercise program complete the regimen.

This program will establish the foundation for eliminating pharmaceutical drugs. After you have become accustomed to it, make plans with your practitioner to phase out the psychiatric drugs. See *Stress and Natural Healing* (Hobbs, 1997) for a complete program of withdrawal.

Step 2. For any SSRI-family drug, such as Paxil, Prozac, or Zoloft, begin with one-third teaspoon or about two droppersful of St. John's wort tincture in a little water two times daily between meals, or one capsule of standardized extract twice daily, morning and evening.

St. John's Wort: The Mood Enhancing Herb

Step 3. After one month of taking St. John's wort, increase the dosage by one-third and reduce the dose of the pharmaceutical by one-third. Wait another month and decrease the dosage of the drug by another third, and increase the herbs by one-third. The entire changeover process should take three or four months. If you experience unpleasant symptoms, consult your practitioner and readjust your medications or herbs according to recommendations.

It is absolutely necessary to work with a practitioner to oversee this process. The information given here is not meant to substitute for the guidance and care of a professional health-care practitioner; it is information that may assist you in the process of withdrawing from pharmaceuticals. Do not take pharmaceutical antidepressants such as Ativan or Xanax in combination with St. John's wort without the advice of a health-care practitioner.

Other Herbs that Enhance St. John's Wort

The helpful effects of St. John's wort can be enhanced and extended by the use of other herbs. The following conditions can benefit from the use of the designated herbs with St. John's wort.

Sleeping problems. When taking St. John's wort for insomnia, a tea that contains soothing herbs will help you further relax for sleep. Select one or more of the following dried herbs: catnip, lemon balm, chamomile, linden, and orange peel. Mix the dried herbs together well, and use a tablespoon of the mix per cup of water for a tea. Simmer the herbs for a few minutes, then steep in a covered pot for fifteen minutes. Strain out the herbs and discard; drink a cup or two of the tea. Add a little licorice or stevia

34

ST. JOHN'S WORT AND HOW TO USE IT

herb for sweetness if desired.

Tinctures of valerian, passion flower, or kava, taken in the evening, also promote drowsiness. Powdered extracts of these herbs in capsule or tablet form have the same effect.

Anxiety. Tincture, capsules, or tablets of valerian or California poppy, when taken in conjunction with St. John's wort, work to relieve anxiety.

Tight muscles. Kava tincture or powdered extract in capsule or tablet form relieves the soreness of tight muscles when taken along with St. John's wort.

Pain. Jamaican dogwood, California poppy, valerian, and the Chinese herb corydalis are good choices for pain relief. Tinctures, tablets, and capsules, taken with St. John's wort, are effective for this purpose.

Irritability. To relieve irritability, the cooling and cleansing liver herbs can be a great help. Select dried dandelion root, burdock root, yellow dock root, artichoke leaf, centaury herb, or wormwood, or a combination, and mix the finely chopped or cut herbs thoroughly. To make a tea, infuse five teaspoons of herbs in one quart of boiling water. Simmer for two to three minutes, cover, and let steep for fifteen to twenty minutes. Drink one cup two or three times daily, before meals. Tinctures of these herbs also work well.

Restlessness. Restlessness is often a symptom of depleted adrenal glands accompanied by a blood-sugar imbalance. To relieve the condition, try a tea or tincture of some of the following herbs: burdock root, the Chinese herb rehmannia, Chinese peony root, and American ginseng root. If symptoms persist, see a qualified health-care practitioner for a total program for health.

Appetite loss (anorexia). The use of "bitter tonics" can help increase appetite, relieve digestive discomfort, and lead to better assimilation of important nutrients, thereby improving overall energy and health. These preparations contain bitter herbs like artichoke leaf, gentian, wormwood, and centaury, blended with warming spicy herbs like ginger, cinnamon, cardamom, and orange peel.

Many commercial brands of bitters are available at natural products stores. To make your own bitters, blend up equal parts of the herbs listed above with 100-proof vodka until creamy. Place the contents in a jar and shake daily for two weeks. Press the liquid out, filter, and store in a cool place out of the direct light. Take 1/2 to 1 teaspoon in a little water just before meals. Bitters are most effective when used for long periods. Many people use them for years with great benefit.

THE SAFETY OF ST. JOHN'S WORT

St. John's wort is very safe when taken in the therapeutic doses recommended in this book. Yet there are a few cautions to consider when taking the herb.

Photosensitivity. People who take large doses of St. John's wort can become overly sensitive to sunlight. Although this effect is well-known in cattle and other animals that graze heavily on St. John's wort, very few actual toxic effects have ever been reported in humans. Patients taking excessive amounts of the extract of the herb, however, sometimes experience rapid sunburning.

Most herbalists and European medical researchers feel that St. John's wort is safe when the recommended dose of 1 to 1.5 milligrams of hypericin a day (one 300-milligram capsule or three droppersful of tincture, three times daily) is not exceeded. This amount of St. John's wort will rarely, if ever, lead to increased sensitivity to light. Remember that St. John's wort has been shown most effective at the dose range of from 0.5 to 1.1 milligrams of hypericin a day; rarely, a double dose containing 2.2 milligrams is beneficial. Taking more does not often bring stronger or quicker healthful effects.

Table 1-1. Foods and Beverages to Avoid When Taking MAO Inhibitors

Foods

Cheese and dairy products

Most, but especially boursault, camembert, cheddar, emmentaler, stilton

Meat and fish

Any unrefrigerated or fermented meats or fish, bologna, pepperoni, salami, summer sausage, caviar; especially beef or chicken liver; dried fishes such as herring

Fruit and vegetables

Avocados, especially overripe; bananas, overripe figs, raisins; overripe fava beans, yeast extracts, sauerkraut, soy sauce, miso soup, tofu

Others

Chocolate

Beverages

Alcoholic beverages

Beers and ales, even nonalcoholic; red wine, especially chianti; sherry

Drinks containing caffeine

Coffee, tea, cola drinks, and others

Although photosensitivity in humans as a result of taking St. John's wort is rare, it makes sense to avoid any possible problem. Thus, if you are taking a therapeutic dose of St. John's wort, avoid prolonged exposure to sunlight, especially if you are fair-skinned. Wear a hat, use sunscreen, and wear protective clothing when outside in the bright sunlight. Do not subject yourself to artificial tanning machines. Very moderate exposure to sunlight, however, should not cause problems.

Cautions in Combining St. John's Wort with MAO Inhibitors

Monoamine oxidase (MAO) and catechol-o-methyltranferase (COMT) are two important enzymes in the central nervous system that metabolize (transform and deactivate) neurotransmitters that are associated with mood, especially serotonin and noradrenaline. Lowered amounts of these two important neurotransmitters are specifically linked with depression, anxiety, insomnia, and other mood disorders. Before the discovery of selective serotonin reuptake inhibitors (SSRIs), MAO inhibitors were an important treatment for depression.

During the last ten years, SSRIs, which are assumed to keep serotonin levels up by preventing them from being deactivated, have become increasingly popular. Today, MAO inhibitors are sometimes used when other drugs for treating depression don't work; they are seldom used as a first treatment.

Certain compounds in St. John's wort have been shown to have a mild MAO-inhibiting effect. These include hypericins, which have a very weak effect; flavonols, which have a weak effect; and xanthones, which have a strong effect.

Overall, the MAO-inhibiting effects of St. John's wort are presently thought to play a very minor role in the herb's antidepressant effect. Although the xanthones are strong MAO inhibitors, they occur in extremely small amounts in St. John's wort. A prominent research group emphasized that the concentrations of the compounds and the overall very weak MAO-inhibiting effects noted in animals (even after large doses of St. John's wort were administered) were insufficient to explain the antidepressive activity of the herb (Bladt & Wagner 1994).

All these factors considered, it is unlikely that St. John's wort will interact with other drugs, foods, or drinks. After more than fifty years of clinical use of St. John's wort for depression, not one report of a hypertensive crisis or other side effect linked with the herb can be found in the literature. One well-respected American herbal practitioner claims to have observed patients' hypertensive crises on several occasions after giving them substantial amounts of St. John's wort, but the report has not been published.

With the rapidly growing clinical use and home use of the herb, it is probably wise to be watchful for possible reactions. According to Bladt and Wagner (1994), a stronger MAO-inhibiting effect of St. John's wort could develop over time, perhaps months. This has been demonstrated with a number of other modern herbal medicines, in which the beneficial activity takes weeks or months to reach full strength.

St. John's wort has also been shown to have a moderately strong COMT-inhibiting effect, but this probably does not play a major role in the overall antidepressant effect of the herb (Thiede & Walper

1994). Researchers currently speculate that several mechanisms and constituent groups are responsible for the antidepressive action of St. John's wort.

St. John's Wort and Certain Foods

People taking MAO inhibitors are required to carefully monitor their food intake and strictly avoid foods that contain the amino acid tyramine, especially certain fermented meats (sausages) and cheeses (camembert, cheddar). If a person taking MAO inhibitors ingests a high-tyramine food, blood pressure can drastically increase, usually within several hours, causing severe headaches, fever, nausea, and vomiting. These hypertensive crises can be fatal.

The following conditions are known contraindications for MAO inhibitors. Because St. John's wort is a very weak MAO inhibitor, these conditions do not mean that you should not take the herb. It is best, however, to consult with a qualified health-care practitioner before beginning a program of St. John's wort.

• Congestive heart failure

• Liver disease

• Abnormal liver function tests

• Severe impairment of kidney function

• Cerebrovascular defects

• Cardiovascular disease (such as arteriosclerosis)

• Hypertension

• Headaches

• Over 60 years of age.

Table 1-1 summarizes the foods and drugs to avoid

with MAO inhibitors. Again, because St. John's wort is a very weak MAO inhibitor and because there has never been a clinical or research report of anyone taking St. John's wort reacting to the foods, this list is given for general information. At this time there is no reason to believe that you should avoid these foods if you are taking St. John's wort. If you are taking more than three tablets of a standardized St. John's wort product (to 0.3 percent hypericin), or more than a teaspoon of the tincture twice daily, you should avoid over-indulging in these foods, just for safety's sake. If you *do* experience headaches with heart palpitations, nausea, or dizziness, especially if it occurs two to four hours after you take St. John's wort, discontinue the product and consult with your herbalist, holistic physician, or health care provider.

Drug Interactions with MAO Inhibitors

Consult your health care practitioner before using St. John's wort with antidepressants such as Prozac and Paxil (SSRIs); diabetes medications such as insulin; stimulant herbal products that contain ephedra, including herbal diet pills or energy-enhancing pills; or L-tryptophan.

Some concerns have also been expressed that St. John's wort may encourage the manic phase of bipolar illness, causing further patient discomfort. No data exist in the literature to confirm this worry.

St. John's wort shows sedative and anxiety-relieving effects instead. My experience indicates that a manic reaction to St. John's wort is unlikely. Commission E monograph on St. John's wort recommends the herb for "anxiety and/or nervous unrest". It does not mention potentiation of mania or elation (Blumenthal 1997).

Liver stress was not noted among animals fed St. John's wort extracts as 5 percent of their total dietary intake for up to 119 days, and the animals' drug-metabolizing enzyme systems were uneffected. These results indicate that therapeutic quantities of the herb are unlikely to interfere with the detoxification or breakdown of various pharmaceutical drugs in the body (Upton 1997). No mutagenic activities of St. John's wort have been detected in any study.

Pregnancy and Breast Feeding

The Botanical Safety Handbook, a publication of the American Herbal Products Association (AHPA), does not advise against using St. John's wort during pregnancy or breast-feeding (McGuffin et al 1997). Very little data exist to indicate that taking the herb during pregnancy may be a problem. ESCOP, however, indicates that preparations of the herb should not be taken during pregnancy without medical advice.

A Brief Review of Safety Studies

In a review of six controlled studies using St. John's wort extract in the treatment of depression, only 0.8 percent of the participants receiving St. John's wort dropped out because of perceived side effects. Three percent in the group receiving standard pharmaceutical drugs for depression dropped out because of side effects (Linde et al 1996). Among those taking St. John's wort, 19.8 percent reported side effects, compared to 35.9 percent of those receiving pharmaceutical drugs. The ESCOP review of St. John's wort reported that no side effects of using St. John's wort were noted among people using products with up to 1 milligram of hypericin a day, which is the typical recommended daily dose.

Researchers found that the skin of volunteers taking 600 milliliters of St. John's wort extract, standardized to 0.3 percent hypericin, three times daily for fifteen days, was noticeably more sensitive to ultraviolet light than that of other volunteers who did not receive the herb. The volunteers taking St. John's wort experienced redness of the skin due to abnormal dilation of blood vessels near the surface (Upton et al 1997).

When toxic symptoms related to increased sensitivity to light symptoms (phototoxicity) do occur, they are described as skin rashes with red, weeping lesions (pruritus and erythema) that develop within twenty-four hours after exposure to ultraviolet light. Anyone taking St. John's wort, even at a typical dose, should avoid sunlight or any other form of ultraviolet light.

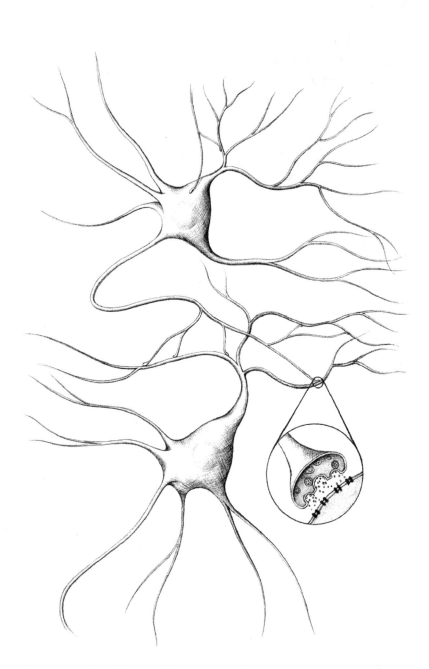

One nerve cell sends a stimulus to another by releasing a neurotransmitter. This hormone binds to the receiving call at special receptor sites (inset), creating a response.

Chapter 2

Depression: What It Is and What It Is Not

✿

Life's ups and downs affect everyone. Suppose a friend cancels dinner plans—that's disappointing. When a friend or family member moves away, or a romance fades, or excitement slips into apathy, it's typical to feel blue, perhaps for several weeks. Sometimes "the blues" set in for no apparent reason. But are any of these downswings of mood really depression?

Depression and other mood disorders are far more widespread than we believed only a few years ago, and science has given us new understandings of the sources of these problems. We know that millions are affected by depression and mood disorders every year; some statistics claim that at any one time, one in five Americans is struggling with depression. We also know that demanding "Get over it!" does not help sufferers; chemical imbalance in the brain, not weakness of character, is often the source of these problems. Instead, treatment is necessary, although individuals respond differently to the treatment options.

Western medicine offers treatments ranging from various forms of talking therapy to pharmaceutical drugs to electroconvulsive therapy (ECT) for dealing with depression and mood disorders. Many questions arise about these therapies, especially if one must make choices for oneself or a family member. Is Freudian or Jungian talking therapy best? How about behavioral therapy? What is the truth about pharmaceutical anti-depressants? They seem effective for some people, but what is the cumulative effect of taking them for ten or twenty years? Isn't ECT what medical people once called "electroshock"?

These choices are confusing, intimidating, and sometimes downright frightening. Is there another way of dealing with depression and mood disorders?

The fabric of emotional life is woven of threads that range from bright and happy to darkly miserable, with many gradations in between. The complex challenges of community, family, work, and personal relationships assure that each person faces stresses and pain along with joys and pleasures. Of course we seek to maximize our pleasure and eliminate the pain, or at least keep it to a minimum.

Furthermore, we live in a time in which cheerfulness and optimism are at a premium. Troubles seem to cover the globe: Daily news reports are replete with information about the deterioration of the environment, growing animosity among various groups, declining morality and commitment to the good of society, and other discouraging news. Internationally, the news is worse as regional wars, famines, and natural disasters bring heart-rending reports. Because so many people feel a sense of helplessness and hopelessness about the state of the world around them, it is not surprising that many feel depressed.

Depression is also not the same as a lack of happiness, although our culture would like to impress us otherwise.

Today, society seems to be saying that if we are not in a peak experience, if we are not young and sexy and experiencing pleasure, if we are not consuming expensive goods and acquiring the objects of our desire, then we cannot achieve happiness. Thus, we must be depressed. This is not so; we all age with greater or lesser grace, experience both discomfort and pleasure, and learn to distinguish what we want from what we need. To be involved in these processes of life, even if they are trying and frustrating, is normal, not a condition of depression. These universal experiences are not the kind of depression that is the subject of this book.

Sometimes we equate depression with a period of grieving or, sadness, and it is true that very stressful events, such as the death of a loved one, can trigger real depression in predisposed individuals. For most people, however, these common emotions are really a part of the everyday life of every individual, normal responses to a loss, disappointment, or defeat. The feelings often turn us inward; we withdraw in order to preserve vital energy and inner reserves to go through the loss, ideally growing stronger, wiser and more mature in the process. This is a time or cycle of inner personal exploration or discovery, or a time of healing.

These human experiences come when they are needed, and they are very much a part of health and they are life-affirming. Life is not a steady state of bliss and rapture, until it is found through the effort, experience, awareness, and assimilation of all human experience, including suffering, sorrow, joy, disappointment, loss, and gain. Depression isn't new to the human race; it's been with us always and traditionally has been treated effectively by healers using St. John's wort and other natural methods. Herbal medicine is a health practice with thousands of years of history. People from all cultures have used and today continue using medicinal plants for health and healing.

CLINICAL DEPRESSION

Clinical depression is the most common psychiatric condition. About twenty-five percent of the patients in public mental institutions and nearly fifty percent of the patients of private psychiatric practices suffer from this health problem. Up to ten percent of all patients who visit their doctors have depression at a level that influences their physical condition (Berkow, 1992).

Fifteen to twenty percent of the population will be afflicted by depression; this means that in the United States alone, at least fifty million people will experience this clinical condition. Of these, as many as sixty percent will recover from the initial episode but later experience a cycle of recurrences.

Women experience depression twice as commonly as men. The reasons for this are not fully known, but some believe that social factors such as the increased likelihood of women taking on a passive role in relationships may be significant. Women also have higher levels of the enzyme that breaks down important mood-affecting neurotransmitters such as monoamine oxidase (MAO); they also experience wider swings in thyroid function throughout their lives. Decreased thyroid activity (hypothyroidism) is ten times more common among women than men. Estrogen may affect the incidence of depression, too; women who use oral contraceptives and hormone-replacement therapy with estrogen sometimes find their moods influenced by the hormones. Finally, women experience monthly changes in hormone levels due to their menstrual cycles and major hormones changes during pregnancy and childbirth.

Major Types of Depression

Depression takes several forms, each with specific characteristics and patterns. The following descriptions are typical of the illness.

Major depression is severe and interferes with many of life's important activities. It can be triggered

Table 2-1. Major Types of Depression

Major depression	Severe depression that interferes with important activities such as work, sleeping, eating, sex, and other pleasant activities; can occur once or several times during a lifetime
Dysthymia	Chronic, long-term depression that interferes with functioning at optimum levels
Bipolar disorder (formerly manic depressive illness)	Often chronic and long-term cycles of depression operating with mania, which is abnormal excitability, elation, and/or irritability
Seasonal affective disorder (SAD)	Episodes of depression that occur during a particular sixty-day period of the year, usually autumn or winter, resolve completely during another sixty-day period, and have recurred at least three times.

by stressful experiences, especially ones that are persistent, or it can occur for no apparent reason. Major depression is likely to recur.

Dysthymia, or "poor mood" is a chronic, long-term depression that prevents functioning at optimum levels. It tends to afflict those struggling with physical disabilities, interpersonal losses, or marital difficulties. Sometimes episodes of severe depression merge into this continuous, low-grade depressed state.

Bipolar disorder (formerly manic depressive illness) is a major psychiatric disorder experienced by only one percent of the population and characterized by episodes of depression, mania, or mixed mood. At any given time, one mood or another may dominate, or aspects of both may be present.

Seasonal affective disorder (SAD) is a depression associated with the shorter days and longer nights of fall and winter. It is believed that the lack of sunshine interferes with the production of sufficient melatonin in the brain, leading to lethargy, depression, social withdrawal, and concentration difficulties. Symptoms typically resolve in the spring and summer.

The Symptoms of Depression

Depression, according to modern medical thinking, is a mood or affective disorder. According to one of the most widely read works about disease in the world, *The Merck Manual* (1992), "moods are sustained emotions; affects, more short-lived expressions" (of feelings). A mood disorder is a condition in which a disturbance in mood becomes a central life issue. Most mood disorders involve different forms and intensities of depression, abnormal

MODERN LIFE AND DEPRESSION:
A CASE STUDY

Sally couldn't put her finger on why she felt depressed. A successful college graduate, she made a good salary, got along with her parents, and had time to spend with her friends. Her fiancé, Ted, was caring, considerate, and looking forward to starting a family, just as Sally was.

At first Sally felt blue, but then she began awakening in the middle of the night, anxious and worried. Tired during the day, she struggled with her work and snapped at everyone. Ashamed, she kept to herself more and more. The loneliness grew, and Sally reached for carbohydrates and chocolate, gradually gaining weight.

At last Sally visited a highly recommended doctor who specialized in mood disorders. Prozac and Valium would solve Sally's problems, the doctor said; but after several months of taking them, Sally didn't consider the drugs a big success. Her mood was not so dark, true, but she didn't feel optimistic, and her sleep was not refreshing. Life was bearable, but not satisfying.

Sally tried to raise her mood and energy by cutting back on coffee and soft drinks and eating more fruits and vegetables. Acupuncture didn't help much, either, and at last Sally gave in to her longings for her morning croissants and cappuccino, giving herself some small pleasure.

Even Sally's dreams of her future married life with Ted became fraught with worry. What if they started a family but something terrible happened? What if their children were killed in a car accident? Over and over Sally imagined how it must feel to learn that her children were dead. Soon she began to tear up at the mere thought of marrying Ted, and sometimes she wept as she thought about her future children.

In a clear moment, Sally realized that her thinking patterns were truly disrupted, and getting worse. Shortly afterward, by chance, Sally clicked into a television show about depression and a new natural medicine that was as effective, or even more effective in some cases, than Prozac, with fewer side effects: St. John's wort. Sally remembered an article about it in *Newsweek*, too.

The next day, Sally called her doctor about St. John's wort; she referred Sally to a holistic doctor. At her first visit with the new doctor, Sally was surprised to be interviewed and examined for over an hour, not the ten or fifteen minutes she usually spent with her regular doctor. Dr. Allen reviewed Sally's health habits and moods as well as her medical history; then she wrote out specific recommendations such as eliminating sugar, except for fruit; phasing out coffee, soft drinks, and other stimulants; and reducing red meat to one meal a week. She also gave Sally a dietary program complete with recipes. It included fresh fruits, vegetables, grains, fish, and especially soy products, which the doctor said would help balance her estrogen. Then came a bottle of liquid herbal formula to support digestion, relax the liver, and calm the nerves.

Finally, Dr. Allen gave Sally a bottle of St. John's wort tincture standardized to 0.3 percent hypericin. Together, Sally and the doctor worked out a program for reducing Sally's Prozac and Valium while increasing St. John's wort.

After several weeks, Sally began to notice a difference.

She felt better, and she kept on with the program. After two more months, Sally was off the Prozac and the Valium. She had some rough spots, especially with changing her diet, but she managed to get through them and change her eating habits. Feeling better than she had in years, Sally began to walk more and soon noticed that her body looked more fit. Developing more spring in her step, she began to go along with Ted when he took his week-end bike rides.

One morning Sally looked in the mirror and was startled by her reflection. Instead of the slightly overweight, sad-looking Sally, she saw a bright-spirited, fit-looking woman who seemed quite in charge of her life. And, indeed, she was, and that life was a happy one.

elation (mania), anxiety, insomnia, and anger. The condition is called unipolar when only depression is experienced, and bipolar when depression alternates with periods of mania or hyperactivity.

A depressed person feels unexcited about life and loses the pleasure once taken in normal activities, even favorite ones. Eating and sleeping habits are disturbed. Energy and vitality drains away, and the person withdraws from the society of co-workers, friends, and family, often becoming uncharacteristically isolated as feelings of profound sadness, loneliness, and guilt become overwhelming. Fearfulness, hopelessness, irritability, and thoughts of death and suicide may occur as well. Relationships at work and at home are often severely affected. Untreated, the illness may progress to suicide.

The person experiencing bipolar disease, once called

Table 2-2: Symptoms of Depression and Mania.

According to the American Psychiatric Association (APA), clinical depression is the probable diagnosis if the patient reports five out of the following symptoms as present for two weeks or more.

The evaluation of depression is often complicated by the patient's use of alcohol and drugs. Many individuals self-medicate with alcohol and drugs to escape depression. Withdrawal from cocaine, speed, and other stimulants can mimic depression.

Poor appetite with weight loss or increased appetite with weight gain

Loss of interest or pleasure in usual activities

Problems with insomnia (sleeping too little) or hypersomnia (sleeping too much)

Depressed mood most of every day

Diminished ability to think or concentrate

Fatigue and low energy

Feelings of worthlessness, inappropriate guilt, self-reproach

Agitation or lethargy observable by others

Recurrent thoughts of death or suicide

The National Institute of Mental Health and the *Merck Manual* (1992) note that the following symptoms characterize depression and mania.

Depression

Depressed mood, irritable, anxious, restless

Crying spells or the inability to cry

Persistent sad, anxious, or "empty" mood

Feelings of negativity, hopelessness, pessimism

Feelings of guilt, worthlessness, low self-esteem, and helplessness; increased dependency

Poor concentration, indecisiveness

Loss of interest or pleasure in hobbies and activities that were once enjoyed, including sex; inability to feel gratified

Insomnia, early-morning awakening, or oversleeping

Appetite and/or weight loss or overeating and weight gain

Decreased energy, fatigue, being "slowed down"
Thoughts of death or suicide; suicide attempts
Difficulty concentrating, remembering, making decisions
Persistent physical symptoms that do not respond to treatment,
such as fatigue, menstrual irregularities, amennorhea,
headaches, digestive disorders, and chronic pain
Possibly hallucinations or paranoia

Mania

Euphoria accompanied by impaired ability to function
Inappropriate irritability
Reduced sleep and not feeling tired; often less than three
hours of sleep per night
Grandiose notions
Increased talking
Disconnected and racing thoughts
Increased sexual desire
Markedly increased energy
Increased impulsiveness
Inappropriate social behavior such as spending sprees and
unusual sexual promiscuity

The APA identifies the following criteria as necessary for diagnosing an episode of mania. A specific period of abnormally elevated or irritable mood accompanied by the inability to function normally.

During that period of disturbance, at least three of the following symptoms are present:

Inflated self-esteem
Much less sleep required
Excessive talking
Racing thoughts
Poor concentration
Excessive indulgence in pleasurable activities, especially those
that can result in unwanted outcomes (spending sprees,
uninhibited and promiscuous sex, erratic and dangerous driving)
Mood disturbance so severe as to impair relationships,
ability to work, or socialize; may progress to the point
where hospitalization is necessary to protect the individual.

manic depressive illness, feels the full force of the symptoms of depression, but these alternate, often on a fairly predictable schedule, with periods of mania; sometimes aspects of both states are present at once. Manic episodes are characterized by elation, hyperactivity, effusive displays of emotion, decreased need for sleep, and lots of energy. Some suffering this illness indulge in wild spending sprees, extremely impulsive behavior, dangerous pleasure-seeking, and other disruptive activities. The change from depressive to manic moods or back can be abrupt.

Periods of clinical depression typically last for six to nine months, although some patients experience episodes that last for up to two years. Bipolar disorder is more disruptive than depression, for periods of depression and mania alternate over periods of three to six months. In rapid-cycling bipolar disorder, a person can experience more than four cycles a year.

A bipolar-disorder diagnosis requires that depression is interrupted by at least one period of abnormal elation. Twenty percent of clinical depression patients eventually develop mania, especially if their episodes begin before the age of 25.

Physical Aspects of Depression

Serotonin is a neurotransmitter manufactured by the body to help transmit nerve impulses, particularly in the brain and other parts of the nervous system. Serotonin is released at the synapses, the tiny spaces between individual nerves and nerve networks; it travels across these spaces to specialized receptors on the next nerve cell, connects with them, and thus stimulates that cell. The serotonin is then metabolized— destroyed by the body—

ending the transmission of the impulse. All this happens faster than we can imagine.

If the nervous system is very active, it uses more serotonin and must create more for the proper function of many body processes, including a healthy emotional and psychological life. When excessive time is spent thinking, worrying, and judging, serotonin and other neurotransmitters get used up. At some point, serotonin levels drop as the body's ability to create them begins to wear out. Then depression, anxiety, and insomnia set in.

At this point, many people try to help themselves by using stimulants such as caffeine and sugar and might feel better for awhile. When these substances fail to work and the symptoms persist, some turn to alcohol or drugs. Others turn to their physicians for help.

Many doctors quickly prescribe a new class of pharmaceutical drugs known as serotonin reuptake inhibitors, or SRRIs, the most popular being Prozac and Zoloft. I have worked with patients who take these drugs; the medications are sometimes useful for helping the individual get through a difficult time. In the long run, though, many patients find that in the end they can use up the last reserves of vital energy.

Depression has physical as well as mental consequences. It can interfere with the function of the immune system, leading to colds, infections, and even cancer. A 1996 study by scientists at the National Institute of Mental Health (NIMH) found that the bone density of depressed women was ten to fifteen percent lower than that of healthy women of the same age, increasing their risk of fracture. The depressed women had an average age of 41, but average bone

The Importance of a Diagnosis and a Total Program for Health

A medical diagnosis is only a part of a total program for mental and spiritual health. Many trained practitioners hold the tools and willingness to support you in finding increased health and awareness. Counselors, social workers, herbalists, naturopaths, acupuncturists, bodyworkers, and religious leaders and spiritual teachers of all kinds may be helpful in your quest.

Proper medical diagnosis is important to understanding the nature of illness according to our present social context. Hand in hand with diagnosis is the need to gain a clear understanding of how to create greater health, wisdom, and maturity in life. The healing process requires self-understanding, support, love, and tools with which to move ahead.

density of a 70-year-old woman (http://www.nih.gov/news/pr/oct96/nimh-16.htm).

Causes of Depression

Heredity plays a role in determining who is afflicted by depression and bipolar disorder; those born into such families are more likely than others to develop it. Family characteristics and habits may also play a role, for early childhood experiences, nutrition, the nature of major life experiences, and other learned factors influence the development of these illnesses.

The most prominent theory about the cause of depression centers on an imbalance in the neurotransmitters of the brain. This imbalance can strongly affect the way we think and feel, the way we experience emotions, and other aspects of our personality. In the healthy body, sufficient high-quality serotonin is produced to allow the nervous system to function correctly. If the body produces too little serotonin, or it is for some reason ineffective, depression can occur.

Experiences also influence one's chances of developing depression. Stress and a lowered sense of self-worth seem to aggravate the condition. Events such as a serious loss, chronic illness, relationship problems, financial difficulties, and other stressful events can aggravate an existing illness or trigger an episode. Those facing life-threatening illnesses, such as AIDS or cancer, have higher incidents of depression.

One's personality also can increase or decrease the chances of developing mood disorders. People whose personalities tend toward grumpiness, unhappiness, bad moods, introversion, and insecurity often experience depression. Those who are prone to

guilt and anxiety are subject to the illness as well. Not only are people with these personalities more likely to become ill, they also recover more slowly than those who make a habit of looking on the bright side of life.

MEDICAL APPROACHES TO DEPRESSION AND BIPOLAR DISORDER

If you feel you might have a mood disorder, and you are commonly depressed, especially if the depression lasts longer than one might expect after a stressful period, it is important to see a physician or psychiatrist for a diagnosis. This is especially true if you have had thoughts of death or suicide. The people closest to you, the very ones you love most, can be badly hurt by the behaviors and attitudes that depression brings.

Those who suffer from mood disorders have difficulty thinking clearly and become confused easily. Denial about the nature or severity of the disorder often plays a big part, too; no one wants to have a mental illness, and many resist even a hint that they are not functioning well. Nonetheless, it's essential to reach out and talk with loved ones and people who are well-trained in promoting the health of the entire body, mind, and spirit in order to gain a broader perspective of the situation and act accordingly.

Diagnosing Mood Disorders

To diagnose or rule out mood disorder, a physician or psychiatrist will interview you about your health habits, drugs you may be taking, moods, and your feelings and how they affect your life and those of your family and associates. You may need blood tests, like a thyrotropin releasing hormone (TRH) stimulation test to evaluate thyroid function, because thyroid imbalance can cause symptoms somewhat like those of depression. An electroencephalogram (EEG) may be used to monitor your brain waves, especially during different phases of your sleep.

These tests and interviews help the practitioner determine if you have a mood disorder that follows a typical course or pattern. Although each individual is unique in responding to various treatments, the practitioner draws upon information compiled by the experiences of many others in determining treatment, the likely progression of the illness, and the probable outcomes.

If your primary-care physician believes that you may be suffering from a mood disorder, you will likely be referred to a specialist in preventing, diagnosing, and treating mental disorders, a psychiatrist.

Table 2-3: Factors that Promote the Development of Mood Disorders.

According to the *Merck Manual (1992)*, the following factors promote the development of depression or bipolar illness in some individuals.

Possible Factors in Depression

Steroidal contraceptives

Pharmaceutical drugs such as reserpine, α–methyldopa, β–blockers

Exposure to anticholinesterase insecticides

Withdrawal from amphetamines or other stimulants

Exposure to toxic levels of mercury

Infections such as tertiary syphilis, influenza, viral pneumonia, viral hepatitis, mononucleosis, AIDS, tuberculosis

Hormonal imbalances such as hypo- and hyperthyroidism, adrenal imbalances (Cushing's disease, Addison's disease), pituitary imbalance, parathyroid imbalance

Autoimmune diseases such as systemic lupus erythematosis

Nervous-system disorders like multiple sclerosis, Parkinson's disease, head trauma, seizures, brain tumors, strokes, sleep apnea

Nutritional deficiencies, especially pellagra and pernicious anemia

Estrangements or separations from loved ones

Cancer

Factors Associated with Episodes of Mania

Pharmaceutical drugs such as corticosteroids, levadopa, bromocriptine, cocaine, amphetamines, methylphenidate, most an-tidepressants including tricyclics, MAO inhibitors, and serotonin enhancers

Infections such as tertiary syphilis, influenza, St. Louis encephalitis

Hormonal imbalances such as hyperthyroidism

Autoimmune diseases, especially lupus

Nervous system disorders like multiple sclerosis, Huntington's chorea, head trauma, complex partial seizures (temporal lobe), diencepyhalic tumors, strokes

Estrangements, separations from, or loss of loved ones

Lack of close friends

Abuse of alcohol or other substances

Psychiatrists must successfully complete medical school plus an additional three-year residency, including both training and practice, focusing on mental disorders. Unlike psychologists, psychiatrists may prescribe, and they are qualified to deal with the physiological aspects of mental disorders.

A complete psychiatric evaluation is designed to assess the existence or absence of specific mental disorders through examination, interviews, and laboratory tests. The interviewer will ask about symptoms, how long they have lasted, and past treatments for depression or other mental disorders. Inquiries will include alcohol or drug use and thoughts about suicide or death. A mental-status test determines whether memory, speech, or thinking processes have been affected; these problems are particularly common in depressive disorders.

Treatment Options from Modern Medicine

In doctors' offices today, patients are often hustled in and hurried out, having spent only a few minutes in the examining room and even fewer with the doctor. Many doctors serve very large practices, and others, pressured by insurance companies and government agencies, seek to contain rising health-care costs by allocating only a few minutes to each patient. The average physician is interrupted in their visit with a patient after only 50 seconds!

Many health-insurance providers cover psychiatric care at a lesser level than physical care. This policy often influences psychiatrists to limit the time spent with each patient. One outcome is that some prescribe medications to help patients when psychotherapy and counseling would be as effective or more effective. If drugs are prescribed, you may end up trying several medications separately or a combination to determine which are most effective for you and cause the least side effects.

Psychotherapy, a useful tool for treating depression, involves regular meetings between the individual and the therapist. During these meetings, goals are established, and the individual discusses current problems and stressors, as well as past experiences. The therapy may focus on developing problem-solving skills, overcoming inappropriate thought patterns, or healing emotional wounds. Psychotherapy may succeed with only a few meetings, or it may continue for months.

A key feature of psychotherapy is the individual's trust in and alliance with the therapist. In searching for a therapist who will be a good fit, talk to friends and get referrals. A brief phone interview

with a short list of possible therapists may yield one or two who are probably suitable. Although psychotherapy costs time and money, it can be invaluable in alleviating depression. By increasing self-understanding and self-management skills, psychotherapy in turn improves relationships, reduces job stress, and enhances recreational pursuits.

The effectiveness of psychotherapy depends upon the client's feelings of emotional safety. Thus, the therapist-client relationship should remain professional, not social. A psychotherapist who socializes with the client's friends can impede the ability of the client to speak freely and feel emotionally safe with the therapist.

Because the relationship between psychotherapist and client is so personal, not all therapists can help all clients. If the client feels no sense of progress after four sessions, then switching to another therapist may be a wise move.

There are many types of psychotherapy. As therapists mature in their work, they tend to improve in the ability to integrate the different approaches to psychotherapy. Two of the more common approaches to psychotherapy are the psychodynamic and the cognitive. Both can be effective in the treatment of depression.

Psychodynamic psychotherapy, sometimes called psychoanalysis or depth psychotherapy, is dominated by the work of Sigmund Freud and Carl Jung. A key goal of this type of therapy is to heal emotional wounds, allowing the free expression of emotion. For instance, a child who was physically or sexually abused is very likely to have emotional scars in the form of hidden rage, frustration, and pain. Psychodynamics theorizes that

the child could not express emotions at the time of the original trauma, and so those emotions form a festering wound that can contribute to ulcers, headache, depression, and other ills.

The second goal of psychodynamics is to replace immature emotional reactions, called "defense mechanisms," with more mature ways of reacting in emotionally-charged situations. Consider a middle-aged man who has suffered from depression throughout his adult life. In working with a therapist, he remembers that a male teacher once made a sexual pass at him. He told his parents, and the next day the teacher was not at school. In fact, no one ever heard anything about the teacher again.

The man realized that as a child he had felt tremendous guilt and responsibility for damaging the teacher's career. As an adult, he realized that the teacher ruined his own career. The man's depression lifted, his energy level rebounded, and for the first time in his adult life he felt free of depression. Such uncovering and healing of festering emotional wounds is a central theme in the psychodynamic approach to therapy.

The other major theme of psychodynamics is the maturation of defensive mechanisms. A defensive mechanism is a pattern of response to a situation. Suppose a man breaks up with his girlfriend and then gets drunk and starts a fight. He's done the same thing since he was in high school: Every time a situation with a woman doesn't work out, he's off to the bar, looking for trouble.

This pattern, or defense mechanism, can be called "acting out." Instead of dealing directly with his feelings of frustration, abandonment, rejection, or loss, the man acts out those feelings impulsively by drinking and fighting, harming himself and others. Perhaps he could learn, in psychotherapy, to respond more constructively by acknowledging his emotions and then decide what to do with them. For instance, instead of starting the cycle by drinking, he could work out at the gym, leading to a healthy relaxation and tiredness rather than a fight. Destructive reactions can be replaced by constructive ones.

Cognitive therapy is the second main type of psychotherapy, an approach defined by the work of Aaron Beck and Albert Ellis. This type of therapy focuses on replacing "irrational" ways of thinking with more "rational" ones.

Imagine that a fellow comes into the office and greets a co-worker. The co-worker, angry that her computer is not working correctly, gives him a grumpy reply and turns away. The puzzled fellow moves on

65

and asks a question of another co-worker. He's feeling irritable because he had a big argument with his daughter that morning, and he has a report due in an hour. That co-worker, too, snarls at the fellow.

"What a rotten day," the fellow thinks. "Everybody is on edge. It's going to be miserable all day." This type of thinking is called magnification or generalization. From one or two interactions, the fellow has drawn an irrational conclusion. If he dwells on it, he may find himself anxious or depressed.

Cognitive therapy encourages the replacement of distorted thinking by a rational approach. The fellow could think to himself, "Those two are sure irritable. I'm glad they usually aren't, and I won't dwell on this. Usually I get along fine with them." Thus he is able to go about his work day without resentment toward his co-workers or blaming himself for the interactions. Replacing irrational thought patterns with more constructive ones can often reduce or even prevent depressive tendencies. *The Feeling Good Handbook* by David Burns is an excellent introduction to cognitive therapy.

Behavioral therapy, the art of using rewards or punishments to shape behavior, is less well-known than psychodynamic and cognitive approaches to psychotherapy. The key here is to sensitively tailor the reward or punishment to the individual and the given situation. For instance, a woman who has trouble getting up in the morning sets a behavioral contract with herself that if she can get up early and walk around the local lake four times in one week, on the weekend she can spend time at her favorite bookstore. This contract works for her in that she finds herself getting up early regularly and getting a lot more done.

Punishments can also be effective. Suppose a man who wants to stop smoking writes out a check for $250 to the politician he hates the most as he smokes his last cigarette. He puts the check in a drawer. If he starts smoking again, he will have to mail this check.

Logotherapy, developed by psychiatrist Victor Frankl, focuses on developing a sense of meaning. Developed from the writing of Transcendalists like Henry David Thoreau and Walt Whitman, who encouraged the pursuit of inspiration, the therapy encourages individuals to cultivate meaning and inspiration in their lives. For many who devote time and effort to this goal, improved mood is one of the rewards. For example, a woman who has long suffered from depression mentions to her therapist that she has always wanted to open a tailoring shop. With much planning and effort, she succeeds in establishing her business. In the process, her long-standing depression clears. Encouraging clients to develop their lifelong dreams and to pursue them can be a central theme in this kind of psychotherapy.

Relaxation training is a component of many kinds of psychotherapy. Most people with depression also suffer from anxiety. For some individuals, gaining control over anxiety can markedly reduce depression. Anxiety often arises due to low self-esteem or poor problem-solving skills, so cognitive therapy and improved problem-solving skills often help curb it. Anxiety can also stem from an inability to relax deeply. Many skills that promote deep relaxation, among them guided imagery, self-hypnosis, and meditation, can be learned.

Although psychotherapists have many helpful

skills, perhaps the most important is the ability to listen well. The client's sense of being heard is the foundation of the trust and alliance between therapist and client. In addition, the art of good listening can be the cornerstone of healthy intimacy with a partner, good friendships, and good business practices.

This art of listening involves neutral responses, such as saying, "Uh-huh" or "Can you tell me more?" at appropriate times. It entails open-ended questions such as "How are you doing?" or "How are you feeling?" or "What can you do about your concerns?" Listening involves paraphrasing; the listener briefly summarizes what the speaker has said with a comment like, "You are upset about what your wife did, and you are unsure how to respond."

Good listening also involves avoiding judgments and interpretations and instead helps the speaker de-velop his or her own judgment and interpretation. An example of listening comes from the book *Siddhartha* by Hermann Hesse. This example occurs when Siddhartha, in his travels, comes across Vasudeva, a river boatman, to whom he pours out his heart and soul:

Vasudeva listened [to Siddhartha] with great attention; he heard all about his origin and childhood, about his studies, his seekings, his pleasures and needs. It was one of the ferryman's greatest virtues that, like few people, he knew how to listen. Without his saying a word, the speaker felt that Vasudeva took in every word, quietly, expectantly, that he missed nothing. He did not await anything with impatience and gave

*neither praise nor blame—
he only listened. Siddhartha
felt how wonderful it was to
have such a listener who
could be absorbed in another
person's life, his strivings,
his sorrow.*

*As he went on speaking
and Vasudeva listened to
him with a serene face,
Siddhartha was more keen-
ly aware than ever of
Vasudeva's attentiveness.
He felt his troubles, his
anxieties and his secret
hopes flow across to him and
then return again.
Disclosing his wound to this
listener was the same as
bathing in the river, until
it became cool and one with
the river.*

Psychotherapy can be in-valuable for treating depression. Pschodynamic therapy is used to help heal emotional wounds of the past. Cognitive therapy is em-ployed to improve the quality of thinking. Behavioral therapy improves behavior. Meaning is pursued to help guide the client toward purposeful goals. Relaxation training helps to overcome anxiety. Finally, listening binds all of these approaches to the very root of healing.

Antidepressant Medications

Antidepressants are not for everyone, but for some patients they are incredibly effective, even life-saving. In clinical studies, all antidepressants have about the same ability to help the depressed, so the choice of antidepressant for a particular individual usually depends on other factors, such as possible side effects, cost, or potential drug interactions. For instance, Prozac can increase the possibility of heart damage from Seldane, a prescription drug for allergies.

The side effects of antidepressants should be care-

fully monitored by the prescribing physician because
the drugs take effect slowly
and side effects can be severe. All antidepressants require about three weeks to
take effect, a long time for
someone suffering from depression; such a patient
often needs physician support while enduring the
wait. With careful monitoring, most adverse side effects can be reduced or
eliminated.

Of the many antidepres-
sants available, doctors
often choose selective seratonin reuptake inhibitors
(SSRIs) for their clients.
SSRIs can not only im-
prove mood but can be
used to reduce mental
dwelling, which provides
tremendous relief for certain types of anxiety. Although Zoloft, Paxil, and
Prozac cost more than the
older antidepressants, they
can have fewer and milder
side effects such as nausea
and headache, which usually go away over time.

A more serious problem
with the SSRIs is that
clients risk about a 25 percent chance of experiencing
impaired sexuality, with decreased libido and failed or-
gasm. For many individuals,
these sexual side effects can
be treated with additional
medications or by reducing
the dosage. Many people,
however, discontinue the
use of SSRIs in the face of
these shortcomings and
consider a different antidepressant.

Newer antidepressants
include Wellbutrin, Effexor,
and Remaron. Wellbutrin
can cause insomnia and
nervousness, and it can
bring on seizures in those
who are so predisposed. Effexor and Remaron can
cause sedation, and Effexor
also causes nausea. Time is
needed to more completely
understand the value of
these new medications.

The first pharmaceutical
antidepressants, the
MAOIs, are now usually reserved as backup drugs be-

cause they can have very serious interactions with foods and certain drugs. For instance, they can have severe blood pressure elevations with foods that contain tyramine, such as certain alcoholic beverages and aged cheese. They can also react with SSRIs and also TCAs.

The antidepressants have been shown to have marked effects on brain chemistry. The SSRIs enhance seratonin activity; the TCAs enhance norepinephrine activity. The MAOIs also enhance neurotransmitter activity. This enhancement of neurotransmitter activity is hypothesized to explain their antidepressant effects. Yet theories about how these drugs work are still speculative. Although antidepressants are known to help depression, it is unknown if their neurotransmitter enhancement is the reason for helping alleviate depression. The actual

mechanism may involve a wide variety of as yet unstudied effects of these drugs.

Although the exact mechanisms of antidepressants are unknown, their classifications can be very useful. For instance, if an individual is having serious side effects from an SSRI, rather than using a different SSRI, it may be prudent to use another class of drug altogether. This is because drugs in a similar class tend to have similar side-effect profiles.

In summary, antidepressants can be miracle drugs for some individuals. Nevertheless, the cost, the potential side effects, and the fact that they do not work for everyone all limit their use.

In today's modern societies, psychiatrists and other physicians are often overwhelmed by too many patients. Additionally, insurance companies and government agencies want to contain rising health care costs and so will often try and limit the time you spend with a psychiatrist. Because of these pressures, a psychiatrist will often prescribe medications where psychotherapy and counseling would be as effective or more effective.

Because drugs are, in essence, the first line of defense against depression, I summarize the most commonly-prescribed medications in the next sections.

A physician or psychiatrist is likely to try several

What If Beethoven and Van Gogh Had Taken Prozac?

The controversy swirls around drugs that alter mood and even personality. Under what circumstances should they be used, and by whom?

Millions are regularly using selective serotonin reuptake inhibitors (SSRIs) like Prozac and Zoloft. These drugs *can* help some cope with depression, and for those who experience recurrent depression, long-term use is common. For others, the drugs are used to make emotional lows less low, and the highs less high.

Perhaps these effects are good for some people, but how do these drugs affect one's creative process? Aren't some of the world's greatest works of art born from times of personal struggle, great inner upheaval, depression, and elation?

What if Beethoven and Van Gogh took Prozac? Would the world have ever known the Ninth Symphony and *Starry Night?*

Perhaps we will soon learn if nature's more gentle mood-regulating herbs like St. John's wort can help ease pathological depression while leaving the creative process intact. As an herbalist I'm biased—and optimistic.

medications or combination of medications to determine which are most effective with the least side effects.

ECT Therapy

Electroconvulsive therapy is reserved for very serious cases of depression in which milder measures are ineffective or inappropriate for the particular patient. These situations include intense mixed-state bipolar illness, a severe bipolar episode occurring in the first trimester of pregnancy, agitated and/or delusional depression, and persistent suicidal ideas along with lack of family support. This therapy may also be appropriate for the frail, depressed elderly; those with depression concurrent with severe cardiovascular disease; and certain kinds of physical debilitation.

The current electroconvulsive therapy differs greatly from the old electroshock therapy so horrifically depicted in the popular culture. Patients preparing for ECT are given muscle relaxants to prevent painful jerking and spasms, and the use of precise technology allows far greater control of the electric current entering the brain. Properly used, ECT has aided many in recovering from mental disorders.

NATURAL HEALING AND DEPRESSION

You are unlike any other individual. That is why a medical diagnosis, though valuable, is only one step toward greater health and understanding of your ailment. The uniqueness of each person is a major consideration in traditional medicine such as Traditional Chinese Medicine and Ayurveda, and practitioners trained in these approaches to healing will approach diagnosis with a concern for your fundamental constitutional type and present energetic condition as well as your symptoms. From this information, the practitioner can work with you to design a natural program that can provide much greater insights into health and personal growth than an understanding of biochemistry and pathology can provide. For the sake of individuals who are in need of healing, practitioners of modern medicine and practitioners of holistic or traditional medicine should reach out and work together. We have much to learn from one another.

In the view of traditional medicine, if a person is depressed and withdrawn, it is usually because of insufficient vital energy. Some of the medications used by Western medicine to treat such a state eventually make it worse; SRRIs, for instance, contain chemicals that reach down into the deep recesses of the nervous system to ancestral vitality and deplete this reserve in order to relieve

fatigue, depression, and anxiety. In effect, the precious ancestral gift of vitality is being used up.

The powerful drugs used by Western medicine are most helpful when they are used with extreme caution for short periods of time as a part of a total program for health. Such a program includes tonic herbs, a strengthening diet, plenty of rest and relaxation, digestive enhancement, meditation, stress release, and proper breathing. The patient must also devote time and energy to learning what situations brought about the depression in the first place.

It is also important to pay attention to the health of the liver, the organ that regulates the emotions. If the liver becomes hyperactive from the use of stimulants or a state of overexcitability, it can allow the indulgence of a continual outpouring of strong emotions. This burns up the

"Yin," the hormones, neurotransmitters, and fluids of the body.

St. John's Wort's Ancient Promise

For over 2,000 years, St. John's wort has been associated with protection against illness and madness. Called *Fuga Dæmonum* in ancient times, the plant was believed a shield against the unseen, evil spirits that were believed to cause these difficulties. The effective uses of St. John's wort were widely known and recorded by writers of the times.

Dioscorides, the renowned herbalist to Nero who lived and traveled in the Roman army, wrote in his *De Materia Medica (About Medicinal Substances)* in the first century A.D. that St. John's wort cures sciatica. Externally, he noted, "smeared on it is good for Ambusta" (burns).

The ancients may have associated St. John's wort with injuries and blood because of the almost magical blood-red color that is released from the yellow and green flower buds when they are squeezed. This association of some prominent feature of a plant, like color or the shape of its flowers, was called the "doctrine of signatures". Long ago, the plant's action in easing mental disorders was also recognized: In Latin, the plant is called *Yperikon*. The name may be derived from *hyper* (above) and *ikon* (an apparition) because of its reputed power to tame delusions or hallucinations (Barton & Castle 1838).

During the Middle Ages, *Yperikon* became associated with St. John the Baptist, probably because the plant flowers in midsummer, near St. John's Day (June 24). During the Middle Ages and Renaissance, the herb was traditionally harvested on the eve of the Festival of St. John and hung around windows and doors, or even carried on the person, as protection against evil. One historical observer wrote that "on the vigil of St. John the Baptist, every man's door being shadowed with green birch, long fennel, St. John's wort, or pine, white lilies, and such like, garnished upon with garlands of beautiful flowers, had also lamps of glass, with oil burning in them all night."

Writers of the seventeenth through nineteenth centuries mention St. John's wort most frequently as helpful in speeding healing and relieving the pain of wounds, burns, and other external injuries, easing the symptoms of rheumatism, and soothing sore and inflamed throats when prepared as a gargle (Barton & Castle 1838; Lindley 1838).

European herbalists and doctors of this century began investigations of St. John's wort, reasoning that its medicinal benefits might be clarified by chemistry, pharmacology, and medical studies. Dr. Daniel reported first using St. John's wort for depression in 1935; for twelve years he had treated patients with "exogenous and endogenous depressions" with the herb (Spaich, 1978).

Over the next fifty years, German researchers performed a number of credible, controlled studies on patients with mood disorders, showing that St. John's wort can be as effective as pharmaceutical drugs in treating them. Further, very few side effects emerged from the studies. In 1997, major newspaper and magazine articles, as well as television shows, have reported on the herb's beneficial effects for treating depression. Today, the unseen spirits of old find their equivalents in microscopic pathogens and imbalances in brain chemistry, and scientific studies as well as long use have verified that St. John's wort can protect against these contemporary demons.

The Stress Connection

Depression and stress are quite likely related. Epinephrine (adrenaline) is produced by the adrenal glands, located atop the kidneys. Under stress or threat of danger, the brain signals the adrenal glands to secrete more epinephrine into the blood, stimulating the sympathetic nervous system. The adrenal glands also link the hormonal, nervous, and immune systems and secrete other types of hormones, such as corticosteroids, that strongly influence immune function.

Chronic activation of the adrenal glands, which occurs under stress, can eventually deplete the immune system and shunt blood away from the digestive tract, impairing nutrition and decreasing vitality. It may also lead to high blood pressure and the inherent problems that derive from this condition. Holistic treatment programs to support the adrenal glands may

be a defense against these actions.

Adrenal weakness (or adrenal burnout) often leads to depression, as well as nervousness and sleep disorders, because insufficient energy circulates in the body. Insomnia can be brought on by overwork, emotional and mental strain, and stress. All of these factors can weaken the adrenal system, leading to a hormonal imbalance that interferes with proper sleep. Without the energy to contain and direct them, the emotions and the mind may get out of balance and mood disorders, along with fatigue, can be the result. This is known as "adrenal fatigue syndrome". Table 2-4 details the herbs and foods that support the adrenal glands.

Dietary Factors

A number of important neurotransmitters that are integral in enhancing or modulating nerve function are built from common molecules found in foods.

Table 2-4. Adrenal and Hormonal Tonics	
Rehmannia	Strengthens adrenals
Eleuthero	Acts as an adaptogen, regulates adrenals, helps relieve stress
American ginseng	Tonifies adrenals and hormones
Chinese wild yam	Tonifies digestion and hormones
Kudzu	Acts as a hormonal tonic
Reishi	Strengthens immunity, regulates hormones, protects heart, calms mind
Aduki beans	Nourish adrenals
Yams	Nourish, strengthen digestive organs

These neurotransmitters are amino acids which make up proteins. An example is serotonin, which is made by the body from the amino acid L-tryptophan, which is found in soy products, dairy products, and meat.

Table 2-4 summarizes information about some of the important herbal tonics that have been shown to help with such stress-related symptoms as anxiety, depression, and insomnia. Many are available in pure form in natural products stores. Consult a qualified natural health practitioner before undertaking a regime of pure amino-acid supplementation for extended periods, because emphasizing a pure amino acid could interfere with the uptake of others, creating a nervous-system imbalance. Experimenting with foods as sources of amino acids, however, is unlikely to lead to an imbalance when a normal, healthy diet is followed.

Depression and its symptoms may be eased by including in the diet more vegetables—especially dark, leafy greens—more fruits, and more whole grains. Keeping fats to a minimum helps, too. Vitamin deficiencies associated with depression include biotin, calcium, copper, iron, folic acid, niacin, pantothenic acid, potassium, pyridoxine, thiamine, Vitamin C, and B12 (Werbach, 1987).

Calmatives are herbs that reduce anxiety and have a calming effect on the central nervous system. They help relax both the mind and the emotions and can be used in herbal formulas for nervousness, sleeplessness, and mild anxiety. Table 2-5 gives herbs that help relieve the anxiety that often accompanies depression.

Table 2-5: Calmative Herbs

Herb	Action	Uses	Dosage
California poppy	Anxiolytic, analgesic, antispasmodic, sedative	Tense muscles, insomnia, mild anxiety	Tincture: 4 droppersful 3-4 x daily as needed
Valerian	Sedative, antispasmodic	Emotional stress, muscle pain, tension headaches, insomnia, nervousness, and restlessness	Tincture: 2-5 droppersful 2-3 x daily; tea: 1 cup as needed
Hops	Sedative, anxiolytic	Hysteria, restlessness, and sleep disturbances	Tincture: 2-5 droppersful 2-3 x daily; tea: 1 cup as needed
Passion flower	Sedative, anxiolytic	Insomnia caused by mental worry, nightmares, and hysteria; anxiety; nervous disorder in children	Tincture: 30-60 drops 3-4 x daily; tea: 1 cup 3 x daily

Life's challenges, combined with a poor diet and lack of relaxation, can lead to anxiety and insomnia.

CHAPTER 3

THE SHADOWS OF DEPRESSION: ANXIETY AND INSOMNIA

❧

DEPRESSION, unfortu-
nately, is often accom-
panied by two symptoms
that are very uncomfort-
able. These are anxiety and
insomnia, and treating them
is as important to the patient's well-being as treating
the depression itself.

ANXIETY

Most people, at one time
or another, have experi-
enced at least mild anxiety,
and some reach a truly dis-
tressing level of anxiety at
least once. Mild anxiety is
familiar to almost everyone.
We experience these feel-
ings during times of stress

such as an illness, a test, or
a visit to the doctor.

More severe anxiety is
characterized by chronic
impatience and irritability,
insomnia, difficulty concentrating, and fear; these
symptoms are experienced
by fewer than five percent
of the population (Berkow
1982) but are so uncom-
fortable that patients may
turn to drug abuse to avoid
them. For many, anxiety
also includes excessive
worry accompanied by a variety of physical symptoms
such as tightening of the
chest, upset stomach, diarrhea, perspiration, dry
mouth, dizziness, increased

heart rate, rapid breathing, and muscle tension.

The symptoms of anxiety overlap those of depression, and as the cycle deepens many patients experience the tumult of insomnia, loss of sexual drive, guilt, indecisiveness, and thoughts of death and suicide without being able separate these symptoms from their sources. This increases the importance of accurate diagnosis and treatment of the patient's problems.

The roots of anxiety and simple nervousness are not the same. People who suffer from anxiety disorders experience both the physical and emotional symptoms of fear without being able to identify the reason they feel that way. Those feeling nervous, however, are usually able to identify the source of the feeling: "I feel nervous because I have a job interview coming up," or "I feel nervous about finding a new roommate".

The forms of anxiety can be mild, moderate, or severe. In severe cases, individuals will most likely seek ways to relieve the anxiety, whether or not they are aware of the depression that so often accompanies it. Successful medical treatment is crucial, because without it those suffering from anxiety often turn to self-medication using alcohol and drugs, a course that leads to addiction. Such individuals may develop physical difficulties, too, such as high blood pressure and stomach ulcers.

Elimination of anxiety is not always possible, but it can be helped. By better understanding the nature of anxiety, and with a little guidance and support, many individuals can overcome its influences. Others who suffer from mild or severe anxiety can, through treatment, find a level of peace and joy they never dreamed possible.

Causes of Anxiety

The causes of anxiety are varied. A large percentage of people suffering from anxiety are undergoing some form of emotional difficulty, life transition, or a bout with depression. Episodes of anxiety are often provoked by emotional stresses, such as perceived changes in important personal relationships, and if the anxiety does not persist, it can sometimes be helpful in coping with transitions (Rakel 1996). Anxiety can also be aroused and aggravated by habitual use of stimulants, such as coffee, cola drinks, products containing ephedra (ma huang), and refined sugar in excess amounts. These substances raise sympathetic tone and stimulate metabolism, either precipitating an anxiety attack or at least predisposing one to a feeling of uneasiness.

Fortunately, about one-third of people suffering from anxiety disorders recover completely. Most others will find significant relief through psychotherapy and drug therapy. Men have a higher recovery rate than women; recovery is also much more certain among the middle-aged and the elderly of both sexes (Berkow 1982), indicating that life experience comes in handy when dealing with anxiety.

Another cause of anxiety is caffeine, which is widely used in the United States and Europe in the form of coffee, tea, chocolate, and soda. Patients who are suffering from anxiety often improve when they gradually reduce their intake of caffeine.

Medical Treatment

Initially a physician must evaluate the cause of anxiety in a patient. This can be accomplished through the patient's complete medical history, as well as the results of a physical evaluation. Often anxiety is caused by a physical disorder, such as thyroid imbalance or alcohol withdrawal. When this is the case, treating the physical disorder at its root may reduce or eliminate anxiety. Sometimes anxiety is merely the result of stress from work-related, financial, or relationship difficulties. If this is the case, counseling alone may be successful. However, if the anxiety is severe enough, doctors may recommend psychotherapy, relaxation training, and/or medication.

Psychotherapy. This takes time as well as personal and financial commitment, but it can aid in coping with stress and reducing anxiety. Some forms of psychotherapy encourage patients to explore unresolved inner conflicts, the resolution of which can add meaning to their lives. Becoming aware of unhealthy thoughts and replacing them with more positive ones is often an important part of the process. Behav-

ioral therapy uses a system of rewards and punishments to reinforce positive, healthy behavior.

Relaxation Training. This approach to stress reduction involves teaching deep-relaxation methods that enable the individual to gain mastery over anxiety. The various types of relaxation training include progressive muscle relaxation, biofeedback training, guided imagery and visualization, hypnosis, yoga, and meditation. Combinations of these are often used according to individual needs.

Medication. In cases of severe anxiety, some doctors prescribe medication to provide rapid relief for the patient. There are three main types of medication used in this kind of treatment: BuSpar; serotonin enhancers (selective serotonin reuptake inhibitors or SSRIs), such as Prozac and Paxil; and sedative medications in the benzodiazepine family, such as Xanax, Ativan, Librium, and Valium.

Each of these medications causes different effects. Serotonin enhancers increase the serotonin transmission among nerves, which can be helpful in treating anxiety, panic attacks, and obsessive-compulsive disorders. Although they are not addictive, and side effects are often minimal, these medications take up to three weeks to take effect.

BuSpar can be as effective as the benzodiazepines at reducing anxiety, but it can require up to three weeks to take effect. Unlike the Valium-like compounds, BuSpar is not addictive.

The benzodiazepines function quickly, often within an hour, and they are highly addictive. They belong to a class of drugs called anxiolytics, all of which are used to relieve anxiety. Examples include diazepam (Valium), alprazolam (Xanax), and chlor-

diazepoxide hydrochloride (Librium). Like barbiturates, anxiolytics are sedatives and muscle relaxants.

The most significant side effect of anxiolytics is their powerful potential for dependency and addiction. Patients can develop severe dependency in less than a month, and those who do face anxiety much worse than the original when they withdraw from the drug.

Additional side effects of benzodiazepines include drowsiness, confusion, memory loss, hostility, irritability, skin rashes, weight gain, dizziness, and impairment of sexual function. Driving or operating heavy machinery while using these drugs should be avoided, and it is especially dangerous to use anxiolytics with alcohol. In older people, anxiolytics may cause transient excitement.

When benzodiazepine therapy is no longer needed, gradual withdrawal is important. Otherwise, restlessness, irritability, depression, insomnia, nightmares, and even seizures can occur. Use of the smallest effective dose for a two- to four-week period is considered safe. Antianxiety medications should never be the sole treatment for a serious anxiety disorder.

Natural Healing and Anxiety Disorders

A holistic approach to anxiety disorders uses herbal treatments, the practice of the healthy stress-management principles,

psychotherapy, and behavioral therapy. Any treatment of anxiety should begin with the simplest and mildest methods; if needed, more drastic measures can be employed.

For mild anxiety, friendly assurances, a soothing touch, and a safe environment may be all that is needed. If the problem returns, eliminate all stimulants (tea, coffee, chocolate, cola drinks, and refined sugar in excess) from the diet, as well as any drugs that are not absolutely

Calming Tea Blend

Linden flowers, 1 part
Hawthorn flowers, leaves, 1 part
Chamomile, 2 parts
Catnip, 1 part

Lemon balm, 1 part
Wintergreen, 1 part
Stevia herb, 1/4 part

Blend the loose, dried herbs, place in a quart jar for future use, and store out of the direct sunlight in a cool place. Use 1 teaspoon per cup to make a tea. Make 1 quart at a time, adding 1 extra teaspoon "for the pot". Add the herbs to boiled water and cover. Let steep for 20 minutes, strain, and store in the quart jar in the refrigerator. This blend will keep for three days. Pour out one cup, warm it, and drink several times daily or before bedtime as needed.

Calming Herbal Extract

California poppy 30 percent
Kava 10 percent
Valerian 35 percent
Hawthorn 25 percent

Mix herbs well. Use 1 teaspoon herbs for each cup of water when making tea. Simmer herbs for 15 minutes, remove from heat, and steep for 15 minutes.

needed to preserve health or sustain life. It is also important to be aware of the crucial role the liver plays in maintaining emotional balance. Since stimulants may upset the liver, they should be avoided. Adding grains such as basmati or brown rice and millet over a period of several weeks or months may produce a calming and relaxing effect on the liver.

For more persistent or stronger anxiety, add relaxation techniques such as biofeedback, meditation, deep breathing, and/or walking to your program. Along with St. John's wort, consider taking valerian, an excellent herbal sedative that has none of the side effects of Valium. It is especially effective in combination with tincture of passion flower, hops, or California poppy, one of the most effective herbs to relieve mild anxiety. Unlike opium poppy, it contains no narcotic alkaloids and is not habit-forming. California poppy is available in tincture form as a single herb

ST. JOHN'S WORT: THE MOOD ENHANCING HERB

or in combination with other herbs. Take four droppersful three or four times daily as needed.

Relaxation Techniques

There are many different approaches to relaxation, some resembling centuries-old Eastern and Western religious practices of meditation and contemplation. Current effective methods include the following:

Progressive Muscle Relaxation. This technique involves focusing on and relaxing each muscle or group of muscles. Lie in a restful position in a comfortable place. Tense and hold a muscle or muscle group for five or ten seconds until it can be easily identified by slight discomfort. Slowly release the tension, and repeat the process with another muscle or muscle group. Continue until total body relaxation is reached.

Biofeedback Machine. Biofeedback machines monitor one's level of muscle tension. The technique is similar to progressive muscle relaxation, but the machine measures tension levels objectively. Thus the patient sees specific results from relaxation techniques. The biofeedback machine can also be used to reduce overall stress through monitoring physiological systems such as heart, respiration, and skin resistance.

Autogenic training is a technique that uses self-suggestions of warmth and heaviness in the limbs to bring about relaxation.

Hypnosis brings about relaxation and mental calmness.

Meditation and visualization typically involve repeating a neutral word or symbol in a quiet, comfortable environment to bring about a state of tranquillity. Zen, yoga, and transcendental meditation are among the many different methods available.

Guided relaxation uses inspirational audio tapes designed to induce relaxation.

Herbal Treatments

Herbal teas and other preparations have a time-honored place in bringing about relaxation. The most effective herbs in this category are the sedative nervines or calmatives. Table 3-1 summarizes anti-anxiety herbs.

INSOMNIA

Today, insomnia is recognized as a disease which is produced by a wide variety of factors including emotional disorders and upset, physical imbalances, age, environmental factors, and a genetic component. More specifically, the National Sleep Foundation identifies the following factors that contribute to insomnia:

• psychiatric-psychological problems

• pre-existing medical issues

• learned sleeplessness

• poor sleep hygiene

• circadian factors.

To these I have added another category—inherent and constitutional factors—which I believe play an important part in one's ability to sleep.

A majority of insomnia patients are experiencing a lifestyle and/or emotional difficulty that has preceded or coincides with the insomnia. Such problems might include the loss of a loved one; a divorce; loud, unaccustomed noises during the night such as barking dogs or sirens; upsets in biological rhythm produced by changing work hours; or stimulating drugs like coffee or amphetamines. Each factor can contribute to and intensify insomnia.

Table 3-1. Antianxiety herbs

Herb	Temperature	Action	Uses
California poppy	Cool	Anxiolytic	Mild anxiety; insomnia; intestinal, bronchial spasms
Reishi	Warm	Immune, calms spirit	Mild anxiety, adrenal tonic, chronic fatigue, immune disorders
Kava	Hot	Sedative	Muscle cramps, general tension, muscle relaxant
Wild lettuce	Cool	Mild sedative	Mild insomnia, nervousness
Hops	Warm	Antispasmodic	Heart palpitation, mild anxiety, sleeplessness
Valerian	Warm	Anxiolytic	Mild anxiety, sleeplessness, antispasmodic, intestinal spasms

Note: Reishi is most suitable for people with long-standing immune or adrenal weakness.

Some people might experience a stimulating rather than a calming effect from valerian (idiosyncratic reaction), depending on constitutional type and how the valerian is prepared. Generally, fresh valerian roots from the garden, or tinctures that are made from the fresh root, will provide the most useful sedative effect.

Illnesses accompanied by pain and other internal discomfort also interfere with sleep. The problems of both initial insomnia (difficulty in falling asleep) and early-morning awakening are often associated with emotional difficulties such as anxiety and depression.

Insomniacs, people who suffer from insomnia, may have a wide range of symptoms. Although the primary symptom of insomnia is the inability to sleep, the patterns can vary broadly. For example, one insomniac can sleep for several hours, wake up for an hour, and go back to sleep; another may be unable to fall sleep at all. Some insomniacs experience daytime drowsiness, while others do not. Additional symptoms, such as fatigue, depression, lack of energy, and mental alertness, vary from patient to patient. Although it is common that an individual's ability to sleep will diminish with age, this does not mean that the need for sleep also diminishes.

Medical Treatment

When evaluating a patient complaining of insomnia, a doctor is likely to take a medical history and do a physical evaluation. Mental disturbances such as depression can be a consequence of endocrine imbalance and other physical problems. Resolving underlying problems may eliminate recurring insomnia.

If no underlying problem is found, then it is necessary to review and practice sleep-hygiene protocols. If sleep hygiene improvements fail to resolve the insomnia, then relaxation training is suggested. Medication is usually a last resort for treating insomnia.

The mainstream medical community does not consider drug therapy to be the best method of treating insomnia. Many doctors make repeated attempts to cure sleeping disorders before resorting to prescription medication or over-the-counter drugs. Nevertheless, when drug therapy must be used, it should be viewed as temporary treatment by patient and doctor alike. Individuals on anti-insomnia medication should continue with lifestyle and behavioral modification therapies. The goal is to have the patient on medication for as short a time as possible, especially since most of the drugs prescribed for insomnia are addictive and have adverse side effects.

The active ingredients in over-the-counter sleeping aids are central nervous-system (CNS) depressants, which slow the CNS and cause drowsiness. These drugs may help with mild or occasional sleeplessness, but they are not recommended for regular use. Over-the-counter sleep medications are contraindicated for those with glaucoma, peptic ulcer, bronchial asthma, seizures, and prostate enlargement. The most pronounced side effects are "next day drowsiness," increased heart rate, and dry mouth.

The most commonly prescribed drugs for insomnia are benzodiazepines, the same drugs that are used to relieve anxiety. Because these drugs are also sedating, they may be prescribed for the treatment of insomnia. They are extremely effective for inducing sleep, helping reduce the amount of time it takes to fall asleep and the number of times awakening, thus increasing total sleep time.

Benzodiazepines are addictive and can cause dependency; thus they are appropriate for treating transient and short-term insomnia, and they should not be used for more than one month. The smallest effective dose should be taken to avoid side effects which may affect daytime performance.

There are two classes of antidepressant medications, the selective serotonin reuptake inhibitors (SSRIs) such as Prozac (fluoxetine); and tricyclic antidepressants (TCAs) such as amitriptyline. Both are used for the treatment of insomnia, and they are especially effective in treating insomnia related to depression.

When one really understands how sleep medications work and how they affect the mind and body, it is hard to believe that so many people take them. First of all, there is controversy surrounding nearly every sleeping aid on the market. Many, particularly the over-the-counter drugs, are considered ineffective. For example, the antihistamines, such as Sominex and Nytol, were specifically designed to prevent allergic irritation and inflammation caused by the histamine response. The major side effect of these drugs, drowsiness and sedation, brought about the marketing of the drugs to treat insomnia. While these and other sleep-inducing medications may "knock you out," they do not offer healthy, refreshing sleep. They usually interfere with REM sleep, which is the most healing stage.

NATURAL HEALING AND SLEEP DISORDERS

Holistic treatment for insomnia is multifaceted and incorporates many techniques including herbal medicine, vitamin and mineral supplements, lifestyle changes, improved sleep hygiene, massage therapy, behavioral therapy, meditation, diet, exercise, hypnosis, acupuncture, relaxation, guided imagery, and homeopathy. A treatment approach is aimed at resolving the potential causes of insomnia rather than simply providing symptomatic relief.

A detailed sleep history is essential to pinpoint the most likely cause of the insomnia. The patient may benefit from keeping a sleep journal for at least a month, detailing sleeping times, quality of sleep, and sources of sleep disturbance. Answers to the following questions are important:

1. How long have you had a sleep problem?

2. Is sleeplessness a problem every night or only occasionally?

3. Is the problem falling asleep, or staying asleep?

4. Do you go to bed and wake up at regular times?

5. Can you relate sleep problems to causes such as anxiety, change in work shifts, chronic disease, or pain?

6. Is your sleeping space comfortable? Any there

any disturbances (noise or light)?

7. Do you have any special habits or routines before going to bed?

8. How long does it take you to fall asleep?

9. Are you relaxed when you go to sleep?

10. Are you exhausted after a night of sleep?

11. Do you nap during the day? Exercise?

12. Do you drink alcoholic or caffeinated beverages? At what times of the day?

13. Do you smoke or chew tobacco?

Answers to these questions are important in determining a treatment protocol. Many patients merely need to eliminate bad habits, such as eating late at

Table 3-2. Positive Sleep Hygiene

1. *Maintain a regular sleep schedule. Arise at a specific hour each morning, regardless of the previous night's sleep, to help set your biological clock.*

2. *To consolidate and deepen sleep, restrict the amount of sleep to only as much needed to feel refreshed during the following day.*

3. *Exercising regularly helps deepen sleep; however, strenuous exercise should be completed three to four hours before going to bed.*

4. *Arrange the bedroom so that it is a comfortable setting. Insulate it against sound and light by using carpets and curtains; ear plugs and eye masks may be helpful.*

5. *Keep the room at a cool to moderate temperature. Excessive heat disturbs sleep.*

6. *Avoid liquids before going to sleep to minimize nighttime trips to the bathroom.*

7. *If liquids are not a problem, try drinking a small, hot beverage (dairy, rice, or soy milk) at bedtime.*

8. *Avoid alcohol, tobacco, and caffeinated beverages (especially in the evening). Note: Although alcohol may help one fall asleep, it causes subsequent sleep to be fragmented and of poor quality.*

9. *As far as possible, work out family or job problems before going to sleep.*

10. *Use the bedroom for sleeping and sexual activity only.*

11. *If you can't fall asleep, don't get angry at yourself; get up, leave the room, and engage in another activity like reading or stretching.*

12. *Hide the clock if you find yourself waking up to see the time.*

13. *Avoid napping longer than an hour or after 4:00 P.M.*

14. *Turn off the telephone.*

15. *Try a relaxation technique, such as biofeedback, meditation, yoga, progressive muscle relaxation, or massage to prepare the mind and body for sleep (Rakel, 1996).*

night, smoking, and drinking beverages containing caffeine. Others benefit from adjusting their sleeping environment and removing distractions that awaken them during the night. Positive changes in sleep hygiene are potentially more effective than drugs for most sleep disorders. A complete list of these habits, called Positive Sleep Hygiene, may be found in Table 3-2.

Enhancing Serotonin to Eliminate Insomnia

Sleep disorders are sometimes linked with lowered levels of the neurotransmitter serotonin in the brain. Like other neurotransmitters, serotonin is responsible for moving certain types of stimuli from one nerve cell to another. When the serotonin has completed this function, monoamineoxidase (MAO) enzymes quickly clear and recycle it, making way for the system to respond to a new stimulus.

Understanding this cycle is important in treating insomnia, because prior to sleep serotonin levels increase to a certain level, initiating the sleep response. If serotonin levels are insufficient, sleep may not occur or may be disrupted.

One way of trying to normalize serotonin levels is to slow the MAO enzyme's destruction of serotonin. Substances that interfere with the enzyme's action are called monoamineoxidase inhibitors (MAO inhibitors). They prolong the presence of the serotonin, increasing its effectiveness.

St. John's wort may prevent the breakdown of serotonin by blocking the enzymes. Unlike pharmaceutical drugs, St. John's wort produces few side effects.

Another way to normalize serotonin levels is to increase the presence of the amino acid L-tryptophan, which is a raw material for

Table 3-3. Natural Sources of L-Tryptophan

Spirulina, a blue-green algae, is the highest natural source of L-tryptophan. It contains 929 milligrams per 100 grams.

Yeast is second only to spirulina, with about 523 milligrams per 100 grams.

Legumes are generally the highest natural source; cooked soybeans are also a good source, as are tofu and tempeh.

Meats follow after legumes; fish and chicken are very good.

Nuts are next in value after meat; almonds are excellent.

Milk products are mostly very good sources, though they contain only about one-sixth to one tenth the amount of L-tryptophan as soy beans do. Cheese is highest among dairy products. Sheep milk is highest among the milks. Yogurt is lower than milk. Sheep feta may be the healthiest dairy source.

Grains: Quinoa is nearly as high as soy

Vegetables and fruits are usually low in L-tryptophan.

Source: *Bowes & Church's Food Values of Portions Commonly Used,* (16th edition) (Pennington, J.A.T., Ed.).

the manufacture of serotonin. L-tryptophan was widely available in natural product stores for a number of years but was removed from the shelves by the Food and Drug Administration (FDA) because a contaminated batch of genetically engineered product was thought responsible for a number of deaths. Although doctors can legally prescribe L-tryptophan, it is difficult to obtain. Fortunately, L-tryptophan is found in high concentrations in a number of foods (see Table 3-3).

Herbal Treatments for Insomnia

St. John's wort, when used for several months at a

Bedtime Tea

Mix together dried herbs in the following proportion:

Valerian root 3 parts
Linden flowers 2 parts
Kava root 2 parts
Chamomile 2 parts
Catnip 1 part

Make a tea by steeping 1 teaspoon to 1 tablespoon of the mixed herbs in a cup of boiled water for 20 minutes. Strain and drink 1/2 to 1 cup as desired. A little honey, licorice, or stevia herb can make the tea sweeter.

low to moderate dose, can help with some types of chronic insomnia. The herb helps preserve healthy levels of serotonin in the brain, leading to improved sleep in some cases.

Valerian is also an excellent herbal sedative that has none of the negative side effects of Valium and other synthetic sedatives. It works well in combination with other sedative herbs, such as California poppy, skull-cap, hops, and passion flower. Some people find great results with the calming herb kava, and many new types of extracts of kava are available in natural products stores and drug stores. Try several brands if you are not getting the results you want, for not all kava extracts are created equal. My other favorite herbs for insomnia include California poppy, as a calming herb, and reishi, an ancient Chinese herb that can help calm the spirit and nourish the heart. In Traditional Chinese Medicine, the heart system relates to emotional and mental poise.

Finally, adrenal tonic herbs are often essential. Insomnia can be brought on by overwork, emotional and mental strain, and stress. All of these factors can weaken the adrenal system, leading to a hormonal imbalance that interferes with proper sleep. This "adrenal fatigue syndrome" is often accompanied by chronic fatigue and depression. Many of the stress-release and relaxing methods discussed throughout this book also apply to helping insomnia.

A few drops of essential oil of lavender added to a foot bath or regular bath can also have a calming effect. Sleep pillows made of equal parts of hops, lavender, and chamomile and bath salts containing relaxing essential oils help promote sleep. You can make your own, or purchase them in some natural products stores.

Scientific studies, clinical reports, and history of use point to St. John's wort's effectiveness and safety.

CHAPTER 4

ST. JOHN'S WORT: DOES SCIENCE BACK IT UP?

❧

SCIENCE IS opening nature's treasure chest of healing plants and discovering safe, gentle medicines around the world. Some major new discoveries include ginkgo for memory and brain function, milk thistle to protect and support liver health, and ginseng to increase energy and performance.

St. John's wort is one of the herbs being examined by medical researchers. Two thousand years ago St. John's wort was used for nerve pain (sciatica) by Dioscorides, an herbalist associated with Nero's army. A thousand years ago, the herb was a popular household remedy for warding off "evil spirits" and preventing mania and other mood disorders. Fifty years ago, a German doctor began using St. John's wort in his clinic for what we define now as clinical depression—with excellent results. Thus a modern "phytopharmaceutical" or plant-based, natural drug has became an herb recognized for its effectiveness in treating various ailments.

In the late 1930s and early 1940s, the first organized studies of St. John's wort began. In the 1970s, interest increased. The first random, double-blind controlled study was performed in 1979 (Hoffman, 1979). Throughout the 1980s, interest increased, and between 1990 and 1996, twenty-three controlled, double-blind studies were completed (Linde et al 1996).

St. John's wort is rapidly being accepted by the medical community and American news media in part because of these well-designed studies. While researchers emphasize that not every question regarding the use of St. John's wort for depression, anxiety, and insomnia has been answered, most agree that enough is known to use the herb safely and effectively in everyday kinds of mood disorders, especially depression.

Although medical researchers from North America might criticize many of the European studies of St. John's wort for including too few patients, or because testing did not extend for longer periods, a growing international consensus concludes that the herb is worth using in a clinical setting. Continuous successful use of the herb in Europe combined with modern scientific study present convincing evidence of the herb's usefulness.

The momentum carries forward the clinical and laboratory research on St. John's wort. Some new studies focus on answering questions regarding St. John's wort's effects on various types of depression and other mood disorders. Others explore whether the herb can be safely used *with* tricyclic and SSRI antidepressants, and, if so, what benefits accrue. While it is clear that preparations of St. John's wort now sold in natural products stores and drug stores are effective, herbalists and pharmacists alike want to know if other ways of preparing the herb might provide greater potency or better overall effects on mood disorders. In the next few years, science will help us to answers to these important questions.

When evaluating an herbal medicine for effectiveness and safety, three sources of information can be considered:

1. Clinical reports from herbalists, naturopaths, and physicians

2. Placebo-controlled, double-blind studies

3. History of use from ancient times to the present

Of the three sources of information, modern researchers prefer controlled studies and herbalists prefer clinical reports and history of use. However, there is excellent information from all three sources on St. John's wort. Written records of the use of the herb go back at least 2,000 years. Physicians and herbalists have been reporting their clinical use of St. John's wort for depression for over fifty years, and controlled studies have been performed for about fifteen years.

Science's View of Depression

The cells in our brain communicate with one another through chemical messengers known as neurotransmitters. Each thought and movement is triggered by a series of signals sent from one nerve cell to another in sequence. One end of the cell receives the message from another cell; it "fires," or releases a chemical from its other end, passing the signal along to the next cell. Once the message has been passed, the neurotransmitter is removed. If it were not, the nerve cells would fire repeatedly. In a nerve cell interacting with a muscle, for instance, this would cause spasms. Eventually such repeated firings are believed to result in cell fatigue and death.

Monoamine oxidase (MAO), and catechol-o-methyltranferase (COMT) are enzymes in the central nervous system that deactivate neurotransmitters, especially serotonin and noradrenaline, that are associated with mood. Manufactured by the human body, their purpose is to break down neurotransmitters such as norepinephrine (adrenaline) and serotonin. Lowered amounts of these two important neurotransmitters are specifically linked with depression, anxiety, insomnia.

The biogenic amine hypothesis of depression, as the medical community calls the theory, holds that depression is due to a reduced amount of serotonin, norepinephrine, and other neurotransmitters. Antidepressant drugs are thought to act to increase the levels of these neurotransmitters in the brain, helping to eliminate the depression.

One hypothesis regarding the cause of endogenous depression is that people who suffer from depression may have less norepinephrine available in their nervous system than others. It's impossible to introduce norepinephrine directly into the nervous system because it does not cross the blood-brain barrier, a layer of tissues that protects the brain from substances in the blood which might be toxic to nerve cells. However, if the MAO enzyme is inhibited by an antidepressant drug, less of the neurotransmitter will be broken down, while the same amount is manufactured within the body's cells. The end result is an increased level of norepinephrine. Antidepressants and SSRIs may also be effective because they block the reuptake of serotonin, norepinephrine, and other neurotransmitters, extending their usefulness.

Recently, this idea has been questioned for a number of reasons. For instance, although neurotransmitter reuptake is blocked in minutes to hours after an antidepressant is taken, the effects of the drug are usually felt in one to four weeks. Some researchers posit that the antidepressant stimulates gradual adaptive changes in norepinephrine- and serotonin-receptor systems. Others suggest that these drugs correct abnormal receptor-neurotransmitter relationships through changes in receptor sensitivity, number, and activity (Cada et al 1997). In the case of St. John's wort extracts, changes in serotonin-receptor activity have been identified (Müller & Rossol 1994).

The central nervous system, which includes the brain and spinal cord, includes a number of "binding sites," or lock-and-key mechanisms where key molecules can interact, initiating a sequence of events that sometimes have dramatic effects. For instance, one set of binding sites are called "benzodiazepine receptors." Molecules that fit into these sites can sedate or depress the activity of the central nervous system. The human body manufactures useful natural benzodiazepines that calm anxiety and emotional upset. Extra benzodiazepines might be produced during strenuous physical exercise, which may be a reason why running and swimming often have such a calming and centering effect on mood, emotions, and mental state. Some scientists have found through laboratory experimentation that a constituent of St. John's wort, amentoflavone, can prevent the binding of benzodiazepines into sites in the central nervous system. Overstimulation of these sites because of a chemical imbalance might contribute to depression (Baureithel 1997).

Evaluating St. John's Wort Scientifically

The first controlled studies on St. John's wort for depression in patient volunteers were performed between 1979 and 1989. In these tests, the herb was combined with other relaxing herbs such as valerian. The studies showed that the combination of herbal calmatives and herbal antidepressants were more effective than a placebo pill.

Other published studies that review the safety and effectiveness of St. John's wort in clinical situations arise from case reports and drug-monitoring studies; more than 5,000 patients were involved with these studies and reports. Although such studies do not meet rigorous international standards for validity and usefulness in the support of a medicine's efficacy and safety, they do significantly add to the assurance that St. John's wort causes no significant side effects after three to eighteen months' use. Many patients in these studies experienced beneficial effects from the herb in relieving depression and related symptoms.

At present, at least twenty-five controlled clinical studies have examined the antidepressive effect of St. John's wort. Nearly 1,800 patients have participated (Nordfors & Harvig 1997; Linde et al 1996). Fifteen of the studies compared the effectiveness of St. John's wort with a group of patients receiving a placebo. Ten of them compared St. John's wort with pharmaceutical antidepressants. Many of these studies were double-blind, placebo-controlled, randomized studies and had reasonable-to-good study design and implementation (Linde, 1996). The studies were performed by various researchers, including psychiatrists in private practice, medical internists, general practitioners, and, in one case, an obstetrician. Appendix A summarizes the various studies.

Considering these studies as a whole, how effective was St. John's wort in reducing symptoms of depression? Some improvement was seen in sixty-one percent of patients who received low doses of the herbal preparation, or about three 300-milligram capsules of a standardized (to 0.3 percent hypericin) extract (about 1.2 milligrams total hypericin). When patients were given two 300-milligram capsules three times daily, seventy-five percent of the patients experienced a significant reduction in symptoms. None of the volunteers in either group knew whether they were receiving St. John's wort or placebo, and, in most cases, neither did the researchers administering the tests. Tables 4-1 and 4-2 summarize beneficial effects and unwanted side effects reported by patients in the controlled studies, case studies, and drug monitoring studies.

A Meta-Analysis of the Studies

In August of 1996 a meta-analysis of twenty-three controlled clinical trials was published in the prestigious *British Medical Journal*, arousing worldwide scientific interest. A meta-analysis is a scientific statistical analysis of a number of diverse studies on a particular treatment in order to determine whether the studies, taken together, report consistent findings.

The meta-analysis of the St. John's wort clinical trials sought to determine whether St. John's wort extracts are more effective than a placebo capsule for treating mild to moderately severe depression, and how St. John's wort extracts compare in effectiveness and safety to standard pharmaceutical preparations for depression. The

Table 4-1. Reported Beneficial Effects of St. John's Wort During Clinical Trials

Most Common Benefits Reported

Reduction in symptoms of depression

Mood enhancement

Improvement of feelings of disinterest in usually enjoyable activities

Improved sleep

Improved concentration

Patients with seasonal affective disorder had symptomatic relief

Symptoms of seasonal affective disorder (SAD) significantly improved when St. John's wort was used with dim-light therapy. Fatigue, depression, anxiety, reduced activity, increased appetite, reduced libido, and increased sleep were improved (Martinez et al 1994)

Other Reported Benefits

Fewer feelings of restlessness

More rapid falling asleep

Longer sleep

Fewer headaches

Less sweating

Reduced gastrointestinal symptoms

Reduced cardiovascular symptoms

Lack of drive improved

Fewer palpitations experienced

Exhaustion improved

Less muscle pain

Table 4-2. All Reported Adverse Effects during St. John's Wort Clinical Trials and Drug Monitoring Reports

Percent of 3,250 cases noted for drug-monitoring reports.

Gastrointestinal Symptoms (0.55 percent total)
Allergic reactions (0.52 percent)
Fatigue (0.4 percent)
Anxiety (0.26 percent)
Dizziness (0.15 percent)
Other side effects such as dry mouth, sleep disturbances, palpitations, weakness (0.55 percent)

Note: Information in tables 4-1 and 4-2 taken from Linde et al, 1996; Hübner et al, 1996; Woelk et al, 1994.

meta-analysis was conducted by researchers associated with a Munich, Germany, university and the San Antonio Hospital in Texas. They found that the St. John's wort extracts given to depressed patients were 250 percent more effective than placebo and slightly more effective than pharmaceutical antidepressants such as imipramine and amitryptiline. Only 0.8 percent of the participants receiving St. John's wort dropped out of the studies because of unpleasant side effects, compared with 3 percent of those receiving standard antidepressants. Because side effects of antidepressant drugs are so common, the researchers emphasized that the studies showed that side effects occurred in fewer than 20 percent of the patients receiving St. John's wort, compared with 52.8 percent of the others. The side effects in patients taking St. John's wort were typically mild and transitory, including nausea, pain,

DEFINING THE TERMS USED IN SCIENTIFIC STUDIES

By Stephen Brown

When studying the effectiveness of any medicine—natural or synthetic—it is important to keep in mind the power of the placebo effect, the positive changes caused by the patient's expectation of improvement, even when the treatment given is known to have no effect on the disease condition. There is an especially high placebo effect when treating the symptoms of benign prostatic hypertrophy (Schulze 1982; Meyhoff 1996; Nickel 1997).

Expectations can also have a significant influence on a physician's or researcher's interpretation of the results of the treatment. The researcher's knowledge that a particular patient has received a treatment can result in a substantial lack of objectivity in the interpretation of the test results. Financial incentives can also compromise objectivity, as in situations where research funding is provided by promoters of a drug under investigation. Attachment to a philosophical position, such as desiring to promote "conventional" medical treatments over "alternative" therapies, can also interfere with objectivity. All too often, negative studies, those that don't produce the desired results, are not published.

In a given test of the effectiveness of a treatment, there are usually at least two groups of subjects: the experimental group, who are given treatment; and the control group, who are not given treatment. The groups are compared to determine the study's results. For this comparison to be valid, the subjects in each group must be as similar as possible in all ways except for the treatment. For example, if all obese people were put in the control group and all thin people in the experimental group, then the comparison between the groups may not be valid because the treatment's effects on obese people might differ from those on thin people. Thus, selection of subjects for a study and their allocation to control or experimental groups must be randomized to eliminate selection bias. Clearly, differences in the populations of different studies can often make difficult the comparison of their results.

Consideration of the above factors motivates the design of what are called randomized, double-blind, placebo-controlled studies. These studies use a process to assure that subjects for control and experimental groups are very similar ex-

cept for the treatment. They are double-blind in that neither patients nor researchers are aware of which subjects received the treatment and which received a placebo until after the test results are evaluated. Such studies have much greater validity than unblinded experiments or open trials that involve no placebo control group for comparison.

The numbers of subjects in a trial are also important. If one were to flip a coin ten times, the chances of getting seven or eight of either heads or tails is actually quite high. With 1,000 flips, the likelihood of being closer to half heads, half tails is much greater. For this reason, trials that involve greater numbers of subjects are more likely to be statistically valid and are given more weight. Differences between the control and experimental groups are more likely to be due to the experimental variable and not to chance alone.

loss of appetite, allergic skin rashes, fatigue, dry mouth, and sleep disturbances. The symptoms were reversed when the St. John's wort was discontinued.

In one review article about St. John's wort, the author writes, "Recent studies have shown that it is clinically effective for the treatment of the symptoms of depression. It has proved superior to placebo, equally effective as standard medication and has a clear advantage over the latter in terms of side effects. It follows that, on the basis of our present knowledge, St. John's wort can be recommended for use as an antidepressant" (Ernst, 1995).

How St. John's Wort Works for Depression

When used as an antidepressant, St. John's wort is taken orally as a tincture, an infusion, or a standardized product manufactured from the herb. For purposes of research, it is necessary to standardize the dose so that valid comparisons can be made. Most clinical studies of St. John's wort have used standardized preparations.

The herb contains a number of chemical compounds that are being investigated for their potential effects on depression. Which of these compounds contribute to the positive effect seen in clinical studies is not yet known. However, hypericin, which has been well defined in terms of its structure and relative content in St. John's wort, is used as a reference to standardize the dose of the herb. Research shows that the levels of hypericin and pseudohypericin in different strains and species of *Hypericum* is strongly related to the levels of amentoflavone and the total content of flavones and biflavonoids (Kartnig et al 1996), and other active compounds in St. John's wort are likely to be found in relatively consistent proportions as well, when compared to hypericin.

These proportions may be altered, however, in various herbal preparations. Manufacturers do not necessarily harvest plants at the same stage in development (i.e., just before bloom), and growing conditions of the plants are not identical. In addition, preparations methods may affect the various other components within the herb differently. Caution, then, is warranted in the interpretation of these results.

Isolated herbal compounds can be tested to determine if and how the compounds creates the positive results in treating illnesses. If the active ingredient can be separated, refined, and concentrated into a standardized dose, some believe, a more effective product can be made. Others believe that the combination of elements found naturally in the plant may work together to produce the healing effect, and that separating them and changing the ratios of the compounds may not bring about improvement.

SPECIFIC STUDIES

In 1984, one group of researchers (Suzuki et. al. 1984) observed that hypericin, one of the chemical compounds found in St. John's wort, acts as a monoamine oxidase (MAO) inhibitor, as do many synthetic antidepressants. Suzuki's group conducted experiments *in vitro* using relatively high concentrations of hypericin. Later analyses of this experiment included the fact that the hypericin content required to cause the MAO inhibition was considerably higher than the saturation level obtainable from oral ingestion of therapeutic doses (Thiede & Walper 1993; Staffeldt et al 1994). Secondly, Suzuki's method for purifying the hypericin had yielded only about eighty percent purity. The remaining twenty percent of the extract was believed to contain both xanthones and flavonoids, other chemicals found in St. John's wort (Bombardelli & Morazzoni 1995); both are considered by other researchers to be more potent MAO inhibitors than hypericin (Demisch et al 1989; Sparenburg et al 1993).

Holtie and Walper, German researchers, used computer modeling to compare the shapes of some of the known chemical molecules found in St. John's wort to the shapes of molecules known to inhibit MAO. They found that the compounds in St. John's wort most likely to be MAO inhibitors are the flavonoids (Holtie & Walper 1993).

Bladt, et al., conducted an experiment in 1994 using improved purification methods to obtain a hypericin extract with 100 percent purity. With this extract, the researchers were unable to demonstrate any MAO inhibition. Using the total-plant extract, however, the researchers found some MAO inhibition, but only at extremely high concentrations in the tissues. The researchers concluded that the proven clinical effects of *Hypericum* could not be attributed to MAO inhibition (Bladt et al 1994).

Other theories about how St. John's wort succeeds in alleviating depression include Thiele's observation that *Hypericum* extract seems to suppress the release of interleukin-6, a cytokine involved in inflammatory response. Suppression of interleukin-6 in turn reduced the amount of the stress hormone cortisol released from the adrenal glands. This mechanism may play a role in St. John's wort's ability to relieve symptoms of depression because the immune system and nervous system are intimately linked on many levels, and a substance that affects the immune system may well have pronounced effects on the nervous system and mood also.

Animal experiments have shown that St. John's wort extracts can interfere with the serotonin receptors on the ends of nerves. The German researchers who performed this work, Müller and Rossol (1994), conclude that "the reduced availability of serotonin receptors" under the influence of St. John's wort might make more serotonin available in the brain, leading to an antidepressant effect.

Some researchers point out that determining the exact mechanism of action for antidepressants is made difficult by the fact that depression is not measurable in laboratory animals (Bombardelli & Morazonni 1995). In truth, the precise mechanisms of action for most of the pharmaceuticals used for psychological disturbances remain unknown;

their efficacy is accepted on the basis of clinical trials.

CONCLUSION

It is important to remember that St. John's wort contains a number of potentially active compounds, not a single purified substance like modern pharmaceutical antidepressants do. This means that St. John's wort may have several effects on the central nervous and immune systems. Herbalists believe that these wide-ranging effects brought about by a variety of compounds, often occurring at modest levels in the plant, are often safer and have more of a regulating effect on the body's many systems than a large dose of a single, purified compound.

Scientists often consider the actions of herbs nebulous and hard to prove, especially since the full action of herbs often develops over weeks or even months.

In this sense, herbs are more like the influence of daily habits over health. Exercise, diet, relaxation, and stress control do not give instant results. Yet eating lots of fresh fruits and vegetables, little red meat, and whole foods certainly extends life and vastly improves the quality of life, an assertion fully supported by scientific studies. Taking St. John's wort might well help improve life as well through easing depression and other mood imbalances, but it might just have a beneficial effect on health and general quality of life.

THE SCIENCE OF GROWING HYPERICUM

More than 400 species of *Hypericum* are known. They occur worldwide as annuals or perennials, and forms include trees, shrubs, and ground covers. Many species are valued as landscape plants.

Cultivated varieties of *Hypericum perforatum* include *angustifolium*, *latifolium*, and *microphyllum*. Each variety differs slightly from the others, but each has the characteristic "perforated" leaves that, when held up to the light, appear to be full of tiny holes.

Hypericum perforatum is hardy in USDA zones 3 through 8. It is a good candidate for a wild garden or a strictly confined one. Poor to average soil suits it well, and the plant is not fussy about soil pH or quantity of moisture. It prefers full sun but will tolerate partial shade.

To plant the seeds, available from nurseries that specialize in herbs, simply press them into moist soil, as germination is slowed if they are covered. The plant grows from 24 to 42 inches tall and spreads to about 24 inches and blooms in mid to late June. It propagates primarily by suckers and reseeding, and stem cuttings can be rooted or root divisions can be taken.

For medicinal purposes, harvest the top twelve inches of the plant when it is heavily budded but only a few blooms are fully open, when active medicinal ingredients are at their height. Processing is best when the plants are fresh. If the plants are to be dried for later use, they should be hung upside down in shade, as sunlight seems to weaken the medicinal constituents.

Because efforts to eliminate natural stands of *Hypericum perforatum* with herbicides, plowing under, and repeated mowing have proved futile, conscientiously monitoring the spread of the plant is wise. Without such care, the plant can escape and establish itself in the wild, crowding out native species and becoming a nuisance.

St. John's Wort

LITERATURE REVIEW OF ST. JOHN'S WORT

🌿

AMONG THE many medicinal herbs used throughout the long history of western cultures, St. John's wort, *Hypericum perforatum* L., has remained one of the most useful. From the time of the ancient Greeks through the Middle Ages, the plant was considered magical and was used to ward off evil and protect against disease. As a practical folk-remedy, it has been used widely to heal wounds, remedy kidney troubles, and alleviate nervous disorders, including insanity.

In the last thirty years, *Hypericum perforatum* has undergone extensive clinical and laboratory testing for its beneficial effects on mood disorders such as depression and anxiety, as well as its strong inhibitory action against the AIDS virus.

BOTANY

Taxonomy and Description

St. John's wort is a member of the genus *Hypericum*, of which there are 400 species worldwide. There is some disagreement as to the plant's family, some placing *Hypericum* in the segregate family Hypericaceae, while others place it in the family Guttiferae. However, most researchers now think that the morphological and chemical differences of the two families are insufficient to justify separating them (Robson 1977; Takhtajan 1980).

The plants are described as glabrous perennials, erect and usually woody at the base. The ovate to linear leaves are sessile, opposite, and well-supplied with translucent glandular dots, which are easily seen when the leaves are held up to the light.

The regular flowers have five short, subequal, entire, imbricate, basally connate sepals and five persistent-withering yellow petals. The ovary is superior, capsicular, and three-styled. The many stamens are arranged in bundles of threes, and the flowers are profuse, arranged in branched cymes which bloom from June until September. In the absence of insect pollination, apomixis (self-pollination) commonly occurs.

St. John's wort should not be confused with rose of sharon *(H. calycinum)*, a common ornamental ground cover in the United States and other countries.

Rose of sharon flowers and leaves are much larger than those of St. John's wort.

Range and Habitat

St. John's wort is native to Europe, West Asia, North Africa, Madeira, and the Azores and is naturalized in many parts of the world, notably North America and Australia (Robson 1977; Takhtajan 1980). The plant spreads rapidly by means of runners or from prodigious seed production and can invade pastures, disturbed sites, dirt roads, the sides of roads and highways, and sparse woods.

In the western United States, St. John's wort is especially prevalent in northern California and southern Oregon, hence one of its common names, Klamath weed. Because of the known photosensitizing properties of the plant, which can be toxic to cows and sheep, it has been considered a pest in some places.

Prior to 1949, St. John's wort covered 2.34 million acres of range land in northern California. Attempts to control the plant with herbicides met with little success (Robson 1977). Biological methods of control proved more effective. In 1946, the leaf-beetles *Chrysolina quadrigemina* Rossi, and to a lesser extent *C. hyperici* Forst, were introduced from Australia, where they fed upon Hypericum. By 1957, northern California's stands of St. John's wort were reduced to only one percent of their original number (Wichtl, 1986).

ORIGIN OF THE NAME

The name *Hypericum* is of ancient origin and may have several derivations. *Yperikon* was first mentioned by Euryphon, a Greek doctor from 288 B.C. (Robson 1977). Pliny called the ground pine *Hyperikon*, though also the plants *chamaepitys* and *corion*. One common explanation for the name *Hypericum* is that it may derive from *hyper* (above) and *ereike* (heather), perhaps because it grew with, but taller than, heather (Robson 1977). Although one Greek species of *Hypericum* resembles heather, it seems more likely that the name derives from hyper (above) and *eikon* (a figure, possibly an unwanted apparition), a name relating to the ancient use of St. John's wort to exorcise evil spirits or influences. The plant may also have been placed over religious icons as a symbol of protection, thus *hypereikon*. Linnaeus, who described the genus, thought this explanation the most likely (Robson 1977).

The common name, St. John's wort, refers to St. John. An important period of the herb's use was the sixth century A.D. when, according to Gaelic tradition, the missionary St. Columba carried with him a piece of St. John's wort as a symbol of his regard for the apostle (Robson 1977). Some early Christian authors claimed that red spots, symbolic of the blood of St. John, appeared on leaves of *Hypericum* spp. on August 29, said to be the anniversary of the saint's beheading. Others considered that the best day to pick the plant was June 24, the day of St. John's Feast at high summer (Fernie 1897). In the Christian tradition, St. John represents light, hence the flowers were taken as a reminder of the sun's bounty (Robson 1977).

History of Use

St. John's wort has long been used by doctors and herbal practitioners for healing burns and other injuries, reducing nerve pain such as sciatica, and for treating mood disorders. It was recommended for "mania" by Prior, an eleventh-century medical

botanist (Pickering 1879), and the first modern clinical use of it was by a German doctor beginning about 1935. St. John's wort's use to relieve nerve pain goes back nearly 2,000 years to the first century A.D. (Gunther, 1933).

The recorded use of St. John's wort began with the ancient Greek physicians. Hippocrates recommended the herb to reduce inflammation and to treat interior sores and lung diseases (Madaus 1938).

Dioscorides (ca. 56 A.D.), the foremost herbalist of the ancient Greeks, mentions four species of *Hypericum*—*Uperikon*, *Askuron*, *Androsaimon*, and *Koris*, all of which he recommends for sciatica, "when drunk with two heim of hydromel (honeywater)." He also claims that it "expels many cholerick excrement, but it must be given continuously, until they be cured, and being smeared on it is good for ambusta (burns)." *H. crispum* and *H. barbatum*, he writes, have "a diuretical facility. . . . and of moving ye menstrua. The seed being drunk for forty days drives away tertians and quartans (fevers occurring every three or four days, possibly malaria)" (Gunther 1933).

Theophrastus recommends *H. lanuginosum*, a Greek species, for external application (Gunther 1933), while Pliny says it should be taken in wine against poisonous reptiles. *H. coris*, another Greek species, was mentioned for its healing properties by Hippocrates and Pliny (Takhtajan 1980). Although many authors attest that the ancients knew *Hypericum* as *Fuga daemonum* and used it to drive away demons, none make reference to specific writers. Dioscorides, Pliny, and Theophrastus do not mention either this name or this use of the plant, but herbalists from the sixteenth and seventeenth centuries mention the name.

Paracelsus, the Swiss physician, wrote in the early 1500s that St. John's wort could be used as an amulet against enchantments and apparitions (Takhtajan 1980). He recommended it for those who have "crazy fantasies" and favored its use for external bruises and especially for healing wounds. He said, "It is not possible to find a better medicine for wounds in any country" (Madaus 1938).

German and other European physicians and herbalists hailed St. John's wort as one of the best remedies to heal all kinds of skin trauma, to stop bleeding, and to promote healing. During the sixteenth through the nineteenth centuries, St. John's wort was widely regarded for healing sciatica, strokes, fevers, urinary bladder stones, and for curing burns and ulcers (Madaus 1938).

Early twentieth-century European doctors recommended the herb as their predecessors had. To the list of conditions for which St. John's wort was thought effective, they added lumbago, gout, headaches, bedwetting in children, jaundice, abdominal gas, and injuries of the nerves. During the first thirty years of the century, St. John's wort became recognized for treating mood and psychological disorders.

Daniel, a German doctor, was the first to report on his years of using St. John's wort in a clinical setting, which began in 1935. He found the herb helpful for patients suffering from "functional psychosis, serious endogenous psychosis, cerebral sclerosis, and depressions of all degrees after concussion." During the next twenty years, a number of other journal articles were published about the use of *Hypericum* for treating depression, notably by Daniel, Bosse, and Weiss (Spaich 1978). Table A-1 summarizes common medical uses of St. John's wort by early twentieth-century doctors in Germany.

While St. John's wort was widely prescribed by medical practitioners for over 2,000 years, it was also widely used by common folks. The plant was prescribed by the wise women for internal use for bleeding before and after delivery (Madaus 1938). The herb was used in pre-Christian religious practices in England, and legends and stories often mentioned it. For instance, bringing the flowers of St. John's wort into the house on a midsummer eve was thought to protect the household from the evil eye or banish witches of wicked intent. Another belief was that if one slept with a piece of the plant under one's pillow on St. John's Eve, "the Saint would appear in a dream, give his blessing, and pre-

Table A-1. Medical Uses of St. John's Wort in Early Twentieth-Century Germany

Nervous system *(both internal and external application)*

Helps heal traumatic injuries, especially those involving the nerves (alternate with arnica, applied externally)

Pain of wounds and scars, especially after operations

Trigeminal neuralgia

Neurasthenia

Hysteria, general restlessness, insomnia

Concussion

Diseases of the spinal cord

Traumatic epilepsy

Tetanus symptoms

Paralysis as a result of concussion or injury to the spinal cord, aid to regenerate nerves, even in paralysis of both legs

Migraine headaches

Hormonal System

Glandular dysfunction

Urinary Tract

Prolapse of the bladder

Respiratory Tract

Phlegm congestion

Liver and Gallbladder

Gallstones

Gynecological Uses

Irregular menstruation

Dysmenorrhea

Endometriosis

Uterine cramps

Alternate with Viscum album for bleeding after menopause

External Uses

Burns, cuts, scrapes, contusions, sprains, strains, itchy and slowly healing wounds, ulcers of the lower leg, sunburn, rheumatic disease, gout, lumbago, hemorrhoids

Note: Information drawn from Madaus (1938) and Spaich (1978).

vent one from dying during the following year" (Alleyne, 1733). The favor St. John's wort enjoyed is well expressed in the following poem (Vickery, 1981):

St. John's wort doth
charm all the witches away.
If gathered at midnight
on the saint's holy day.
And devils and witches
have no power to harm
Those that do gather the
plant for a charm:
Rub the lintels and post
with that red juicy flower
No thunder nor tempest
will then have the power
To hurt or to hinder
your houses: and bind
Round your neck a
charm of a similar kind.

Several noted English herbalists, reflecting the general beliefs of their time, wrote favorably of the virtues of St. John's wort. For instance, Gerard (ca.

1600) tells of the ointment he made of the plant as being a "most precious remedy for deepe wounds," and adds "there is not a better natural balsam . . . to cure any such wound" (1633).

Culpeper (ca. 1650), who was fond of ascribing astrological signs to medicinal herbs, says that *Hypericum* "is under the celestial sign Leo, and the dominion of the Sun," continuing that "it is a singular wound herb, healing inward hurts or bruises," and that as an ointment "it opens obstructions, dissolves swelling, and closes up the lips of wounds." Also, he claims St. John's wort is good for those who "are bitten or stung by any venomous creature, and for those that cannot make water," which use modern science confirms. He adds that the plant helps with "sciatica, the falling sickness, and the palsy" when one drinks a preparation of the seeds boiled in wine (Culpeper 1847).

The flowering tops of *Hypericum* were usually macerated in oil (such as olive oil) and then placed in the sun for two or three weeks, yielding a preparation "esteemed as one of the most popular and curative applications in Europe for excoriations, wounds, and bruises" (Fernie 1897). This preparation was even used by the surgeons to clean foul wounds and was official in the first *London Pharmacopoeia* as *Oleum Hyperici* (State Historical Society of Wisconsin 1944).

Other popular folk uses for St. John's wort have included treating small stones in the kidneys and bladder and ulcerations of the ureter (Hill 1808); ulcerations of the kidneys, fever, worms, jaundice, gout, and rheumatism (Greene 1824); as an infusion (one ounce of herb to one pint water) for chronic catarrhs of the lungs, bowels, or urinary passages; and as a warm lotion on injuries to the spinal cord or injured nerves. Other uses included the treatment of bed sores and the spasmed muscles of tetanus (Fernie 1897). In Germany, "Johanniskraut," as it was called, was considered especially effective for starting the menstrual flow in women whose periods had stopped and to cure uterine disease (Madaus 1938).

In Russia, St. John's wort was also a popular folk remedy, and a number of reports indicate that it was taken internally for relieving back pain, hemorrhoids, pulmonary edema, ulcers, and dysentery. Tartar women drank a decoction for excessive menstrual bleeding. Externally, St. John's wort was used as a compress for curing wounds, bruises, and burns. Russian farmers commonly soaked the herb in vodka or other spirits and drank the brew a few sips at a time to prevent and cure tuberculosis, hemorrhoids, cholera, and many other diseases. An 1869 Russian article reported that a decoction of the herb was a common ingredient in teas for the chest and to promote sweating (Madaus 1938).

The Native Americans used several indigenous species of *Hypericum* as an abortifacient, antidiarrheal, dermatological aid, febrifuge, hemostatic, snake-bite remedy, and general strengthener. After St. John's wort was introduced by European settlers, they used it for similar conditions (Moerman 1986; Vogel 1970).

As for the early United States, St. John's wort was not well-known and was rarely mentioned by prominent writers on the subject of medicinal plants. One of the first references to the plant is by Griffith (1847), who says it can be used as an oil or ointment for ul-cers and tumors and taken internally as a diuretic.

The Eclectics, medical doctors from the late 1800s and early 1900s who favored the use of herbs, did not use St. John's wort extensively, although John King, a noted Eclectic physician, mentions it in his *Dispensatory* (1876). He reports that St. John's wort is useful for urinary affections, diarrhea, worms, jaundice, menorrhagia, hysteria, and nervous imbalance with depression. He also notes external applications including the use of the saturated tincture as a substitute for arnica in treating bruises. In the later Felter-Lloyd revision of King's *Dispensatory*, tincture of St. John's wort in a dose of ten to thirty drops mixed with four ounces of water, taken in teaspoonful doses every one to two hours, is prescribed for spinal irritation, shocks, concussions, puncture wounds, and hysteria (Felter & Lloyd, 1898).

CHEMISTRY

The genus *Hypericum* has a complex and diverse chemical makeup. *H. perforatum* has been most intensively studied, but there is data available on sixty-six other species (Kitanov & Blinova, 1987). The compounds that have been identified from *H. perforatum* can be divided into several classes, which are summarized along with their pharmacological activity in Table A-2.

Hypericin and pseudohypericin are soluble in oil and probably alcohol during exposure to sunlight (Maisenbacher & Kovar 1992). In addition, most hypericin and pseudohypericin compounds are created after the flowering tops are ground or crushed and exposed to sunlight. This explains the traditional method of extraction for St. John's wort mentioned in herbals, but after long exposure the two compounds break down (Wagner & Bladt 1994). Present studies do not determine whether hypericin and pseudohypericin or their breakdown products are more potent as antidepressive agents. Based on my experience, the original compounds are likely to be the most potent.

Constituent levels are influenced by a variety of environmental factors. For instance, the hypericin and tannin content of *H. perforatum* is higher at growth temperatures above 14 degrees C. (tannin, 15.06 percent of dry weight) than below (13.42 percent). Both hyperin and rutin contents are higher in dry conditions (1.25 percent and 2.32 percent respectively) than wet conditions (no figure given and 1.89 percent, respectively). Hyperin content is highest at 7P.M. (Prokosheva & Shatunova 1985). Total tannin content is highest when the buds are forming, just prior to flowering, in June (Gozin &

ST. JOHN'S WORT: THE MOOD ENHANCING HERB

Table A-2. The Antidepressive and Mood-Enhancing Effects of St. John's Wort

Enhancement of the interaction of serotonin and norepinephrine with receptor sites on nerve cells in the brain

Inhibition of key enzymes that break down serotonin, norepinephrine (MAO and COMT), and other neurotransmitters (i.e., GABA) by flavonoids, xanthones, and hypericins

Inhibition of serotonin uptake by postsynaptic receptors

Interaction of hypericin with GABA/benzodiazepine receptors

Reduced number of serotonin receptors on nerve cells might allow increased serotonin availability in the brain

Suppression of interleukin-6 release from immune cells, reducing production of the stress hormone cortisol from the adrenal glands, as seen in blood samples taken from depressive patients taking Hypericum

Note: Information was drawn from ESCOP, 1996; Thiele, 1993; Müller and Rossol, 1994; Bladt et al 1994; Perovic and Muller, 1995.

Yasnetsov 1979; Razinskaite 1970).

Higher amounts of flavonoids, including rutin, quercetin, and hyperin, occur in plants on northern slopes with few generative shoots (Zhebeleva 1973). Flavonoid content (rutin, hyperin, quercetin, and quercitrin) is highest in the leaves of St. John's wort and is at maximum concentration during full bloom. In the flowers, the content of flavonoids is highest at the start of flowering, falling sharply during flowering (Razinskaite 1971). St. John's wort flowers had the highest content of flavonoids (11.71 percent) of any of 223 plant species tested (Tsitsina d.m.).

130

PHARMACOLOGY

Extracts of the flowering tops of *Hypericum perforatum* have shown a variety of effects in the laboratory, including psychotropic activity, wound and burn-healing activity, bactericidal effects against pathogens in pyelitis and cystitis, antiviral effects, sunscreen activity (disputed), antidepressive activity, and diuretic, anthelmintic, and mildly uterotonic activity (Hostettmann & Wagner 1977; Denisova-Dyatlova & Glyzin 1982; Karryev & Komissarenko 1980). Although more work needs to be done to validate the many uses of St. John's wort in clinical and common practice, some laboratory studies corroborate its use for some of these conditions and point the way for further research. Following is a summary of the laboratory work that has been conducted on the pharmacological effects of St. John's wort extract or oil.

Antidepressive and Psychotropic Activity

Among the most common psychiatric illnesses today are depression, mania (abnormal elation with irritability), bipolar affective disorder (characterized by swings between depression and mania), and schizophrenia. One of the best-known but controversial theories hypothesizes that depression is caused by deficiency or decreased effectiveness of norepinephrine and serotonin, neurotransmitters that act as nerve-impulse transmitting substances in particular nerve pathways.

How synthetic and natural antidepressants work in the brain is not fully understood. A number of theories have been put forth about how St. John's wort works; these are summarized in Table A-3. It is possible, even likely, that the plant has multiple pharmacological effects.

In Vitro Experiments

Ethanol and water extracts of *Hypericum* have shown weak monoamine oxidase (MAO)-inhibitory effects (Demisch et al 1989; Sparenberg et al 1993; Thiede & Walper 1993; Bladt & Wagner 1993), and the flavonoid-rich extract, catechol-O-methyl-transferase (COMT) inhibiting-activity (Thiede & Walper 1993).

Interactions with hypericin and GABA/benzodiazepine receptors and serotonin (5-HT1) receptors have also been reported (Curle et al 1988). The biflavone amentoflavone has also been shown to interact with benzodiazepine receptors (Nielsen et al 1988).

Other studies have demonstrated the dopamine-(-hydroxylase-inhibiting effects of hypericin (Obry 1991), a reduced expression of serotonin receptors in a neuroblastoma cell line, and a potent suppression of interleukin-6 release in human blood, from a hydroalcoholic extract of *Hypericum* (Müller et al 1993; Thiele et al 1993).

In Vivo Experiments

A standardized (hypericin) extract of *H. perforatum* has been tested in various animal models generally used for determining antidepressant activity. It has been found to enhance the exploratory activity of mice in a foreign environment, generally increasing physical activity. The extract extends sleeping time dose-dependently, and has shown reserpine (a depressant) antagonism and decreased aggressive behavior in socially isolated male mice after three weeks of treatment with oral doses of a hydroethanolic extract containing 2-12 mg/kg hypericin (Okpanyi & Weishcer 1987).

External applications of *Hypericum* extracts have shown anti-inflammatory and antibacterial effects (Hölzl 1989; Hobbs 1989; Hölzl 1993; Brantner et al 1994), which has been attributed to the hyperforin (Brondz et al 1982). A number of studies have demonstrated the strong antiviral effects of *Hypericum* extracts (Andersen et al 1991; Barnard et al 1992; Hudson et al 1991; Hudson et al 1993; Kraus et al 1990; Lavie et al 1989; Meruelo et al 1988; Schinazi et al 1990; Takahashi et al 1989).

Müldner and Zöller (1984), in a clinical trial with six depressive women, aged 55 to 65, measured metabolites of noradrenaline and dopamine in the urine and found that after taking a standardized hypericin extract, there was a significant increase of 3-methoxy-4-hydroxyphenyl-glucol, a marker for the beginning of an antidepressive reaction. The same research team, working with fifteen women taking a standard hypericin extract, demonstrated an improvement in symptoms of anxiety, dysphoric mood, loss of interest, hypersomnia, anorexia, depression (worse in the morning), insomnia, obstipation, psychomotoric retardation, and feelings of worthlessness. They reported no side effects (von Müldner & Zöller 1984).

Standardized liquid preparations were given orally to six women with depressive symptoms and found to increase the urinary secretion of neurotransmitter metabolites after two hours. The dose contained 0.5 milligrams of hypericin (von Müldner & Zöller 1984). The same preparations was given to forty depressive patients for four weeks, and the brain waves were studied by electroencephalogram (EEG). An increase in theta activity and a decrease in alpha activity was seen, indicating a calming effect. The reduction in alpha-wave levels was far less than that seen with bromazepam (Kugler et al 1990). A further double-blind, placebo-controlled cross-over EEG study with twelve healthy volunteers showed that after six weeks of medication with 900 milligrams of a standardized extract of *Hypericum*, alpha waves were reduced, and theta and beta frequencies increased (Johnson, 1991).

In another group of volunteers, a St. John's wort standardized extract was given in the amount of 300 milligrams, three times daily. The *Hypericum* improved sleep quality and enhanced REM sleep (Schulz & Jobert 1993). The same extract and dose given to twenty-four healthy patients for four weeks showed a tendency to improve cognitive functions, according to researchers (Johnson et al 1993).

One way in which St. John's wort might help improve sleep in depressed patients is by increasing the nocturnal melatonin content of blood plasma. The levels were significantly increased in thirteen healthy volunteers who received a St. John's wort preparation containing 0.53 milligrams of total hypericins for three weeks (Demisch et al 1991).

WOUND AND BURN HEALING

Many cultures have depended on St. John's wort to ease the pain and inflammation of trauma including burns, cuts, abrasions, strains, sprains and pinched nerves. Modern research is now showing, on the molecular and cellular levels, how the herb works for these purposes. Researchers have found that extracts of St. John's wort can suppress the immune response to decrease inflammation, reducing pain and swelling. St. John's wort enhances other aspects of the immune processes, perhaps helping to promote healing. For instance, the tannin or polyphenol fraction can stimulate the mononuclear phagocyte system, the immune cells that remove waste products from blood and tissues. The fat-soluble compounds can reduce other aspects of immunity (Evstifeeva & Sibiriak, 1996).

St. John's wort is also a powerful antioxidant, more potent than many other well-known tonic and protective herbs such as eleuthero, schisandra, and ginseng (Bol'shakova et al, 1997). It is not known whether this effect plays a role in the antidepressive activity of St. John's wort, but it is probably significant in the herb's ability to lower inflammation and pain in burns and injuries.

In a number of studies, St. John's wort extracts have demonstrated antibacterial and wound-healing activity. For instance, two widely prescribed Russian preparations of *Hypericum*, novoimanine and imanine, have been tested against *Staphylococcus aureus* infection *in vivo* and *in vitro* and been found to be more effective than sulfonilamide (Negrash & Pochinok 1972; Aizenman 1969; Derbentseva & Rabinovich 1968). Hyperforin, a bicyclic tetraketone from *H. perforatum*, is reported to be a main antibiotic constituent of novoimanine (Gurevich et al 1971).

One German patent mentions that an ointment containing an extract of St. John's wort flowers shortened healing time of burns and showed antiseptic activity (Saljic 1975). According to the report, first-degree burns healed in forty-eight hours when treated with the ointment, while second- and third-degree burns healed without keloid (a type of scar tissue) formation three times faster than burns treated by conventional methods.

St. John's wort oil was used in commercial products as a sun screen, but reports of its efficacy for this purpose are contradictory (Proserpio 1976; Morelli et al 1983).

Antiviral Effects

International interest increased in St. John's wort after researchers from New York University medical center and the Weizmann Institute of Science in Israel demonstrated that two compounds from the plant strongly inhibit a variety of retroviruses, including the AIDS virus, both *in vitro* and *in vivo* (Menuelo et al 1988). Several points from this report bear citing:

• When the compounds interact with the infecting particles shortly after *in vivo* administration,

disease is completely prevented

• Preliminary in vitro studies with pseudohypericin indicate that it can reduce the spread of HIV.

• The total yield of hypericin and psuedohypericin from *H. triquetrifolium* Turra was 0.04 percent.

• The compounds were still effective when administered orally or interperitoneally within one day of infection.

• No serious toxic side effects were noticed after testing more than 800 mice with the compounds. Administration of the compounds did not result in abnormalities in any of a wide variety of clinical tests performed on the animals.

• Hypericin shows toxicity to some human cells at very high concentrations

(>10 ug/ml, or lower for some cell types). Pseudo-hypericin is less toxic. Fortunately, the compounds show remarkable antiviral potency "after one administration of a relatively small dose of the compounds."

• The compounds directly inactivate the virions or interfere with assembly or shedding of assembled viral particles.

• The compounds can cross the blood-brain barrier.

A number of *in vivo* and *in vitro* laboratory studies have shown that hypericin in St. John's wort extracts actively inhibits murine retroviruses like Friend leukemia virus and radiation-leukemia virus, as well as a ganciclovir-resistant strain of human cytomegalovirus and the human immunodeficiency virus type 1 (HIV-1) in a dose-dependent manner. Only viruses that possess membranes seem to be affected and light powerfully potentiates hypericin's virucidal activity (Weber et al 1994).

The only reports of a long-term treatment trials in human volunteers with AIDS patients is from Germany and Israel (Steinbeck-Klose & Wernet 1993; Vonsover et al 1996). Researchers reported that in an open pilot study with eighteen HIV patients treated solely with a St. John's wort product (Hyperforat at 2 milliliters intravenously twice weekly; plus two tablets, three times daily) showed stable or increasing counts of absolute CD4 T-helper cell levels over the forty months of observation, independent of the beginning levels of these immune cells. Only two patients encountered opportunistic infections during the study. These patients were clinically stable

ST. JOHN'S WORT: THE MOOD ENHANCING HERB

and were able to work while undergoing treatment. No side effects from the St. John's wort were reported.

In another pilot study with eighteen patients who received a St. John's wort regime similar to that mentioned above, patients' plasma viral RNA loads were substantially reduced in most of the p24Ag. positive and negative individuals. Some of the patients were treated for four to six years. The researchers concluded that there was strong evidence to support further trials with hypericin and St. John's wort extracts. Clinical trials are underway as reported in the 8th International Conference on AIDS, July 19-24, 1992, to determine the usefulness of this promising treatment for HIV and AIDS (Lenard et al, 1993).

A standardized extract (to hypericin as a marker compound) may be the surest way to administer the plant for viral therapy, although other compounds are likely to play an important role in the overall antiviral effect of the plant. For this reason, a good quality liquid extract containing a more diverse number of compounds than the standardized powdered extract should be studied for use against HIV/AIDS.

TOXICITY

Besides its long history of use as a medicinal plant, St. John's wort is also known as a photosensitizing plant that can cause sickness and even death when eaten in large amounts by grazing animals such as cattle, sheep, horses, and goats, but also rabbits and rats (Schleel 1972). This toxic activity of St. John's wort was first noted in the literature by Cirillo (1787), and since then many published papers have noted this effect (Marsh, 1930).

The plant, however, does not seem to be a major threat to livestock, because the first symptoms of *Hypericum* intoxication includes loss of appetite, which makes the absorption of the photodynamic pigment, hypericin, self-limiting (Araya & Ford 1981).

In the case of *Hypericum* toxicity, the compound hypericin is absorbed from the intestine and concentrates near the skin. When the skin of the animal is exposed to sunlight, an allergic reaction takes place. Oxygen is necessary for the photodynamic hemolysis (destruction of red blood cells), leading to tissue damage. In the absence of sunlight, a reaction will not occur and the compound does not show particular toxicity (Garrett et al 1982; Pace & MacKinney 1941). This first type of reaction is called primary photosensitization (Clare 1952). Another, more serious. type is secondary photosensitization, in which the liver and other internal organs can be damaged (James & Johnson 1976).

Cattle appear to be more sensitive to the phototoxicity of hypericin than sheep. In one test with cattle, a single dose of one gram per kilo of body weight of dried *Hypericum* showed no photosensitization or changes in liver enzymes, but three or four times that amount did. If humans were as sensitive to hypericin as cattle, this dose would correlate to fifty-nine grams of freshly dried herb for a 130-pound individual. Importantly, hypericin does not seem to be accumulative (Araya & Ford 1981). Although a considerable number of published studies have demonstrated the phototoxicity of hypericin in various animal species (Zaichikova et al 1985; Roth et al 1920), a thorough search brings to light only a few cases involving human toxicity.

The German doctor and herbalist Rudolph Weiss

recommends caution when using large quantities of St. John's wort extract for medicinal uses, particularly for people with fair skin, who should not expose themselves to strong sunlight during *Hypericum* therapy (Weiss 1988). Judging by the available literature, a very moderate daily dose, up to four grams of the dried herb, three to ten milliliters of the 1:5 tincture (40 percent EtOH), or 900 milligrams of the powdered extract, (standardized to 0.3 percent hypericin), daily should not pose a problem if sunlight restriction is followed (*Merck Index* 1907; Todd 1967), especially given the widespread use of *H. perforatum* extracts in Europe.

In one double-blind study, up to one milligram of hypericin daily for eight days was given to forty volunteers, and phototoxicity was not observed (Wienert et al 1991). When hypericin was injected into HIV-in-fected patients, symptoms of phototoxicity were seen at the equivalent of thirty-five times the normal therapeutic dose (James 1992).

In a series of animal and *in vitro* laboratory tests, no mutagenic, or genotoxic effects of various liquid extracts of *Hypericum* were seen (ESCOP 1996). An extensive review of the toxicity of St. John's wort is available (Upton 1997).

Identification and Adulteration

For identification of cut and sifted material from the commercial drug market, note the two opposite ridges on the stems. These are prominent and an important characteristic in differentiating *Hypericum* species.

Ideally, the commercial drug should consist mostly of flowering tops, but in common practice the whole above-ground plant with a considerable quantity of stem may be present. At least seventy to ninety percent of the flowers that are present should consist of immature capsules; otherwise the plants may have been harvested too late in the season. The hypericin content declines immediately after flower maturity and pollination.

The leaves, when observed with a 10X hand lens, can be characterized by many punctate glands, or very small, somewhat transparent dots, clearly distinguishable by holding them up to a light source. The flowers will all contain fragments of the persistent dried petals, which may have red glands (appearing black) around the perimeter.

St. John's wort has a characteristically resinous, slightly bitter, pungent, and astringent taste and smell due partly to its essential oil. A commercial oil or tincture of *Hypericum* should be vivid, almost fluorescent red. If any liquid preparation of the herb, either oil or tincture, is pale red to pink, the hypericin content, and thus the quality of the product, is suspect. In my experience, the extract or oil should be dark red for maximum effectiveness.

Several methods are given in the literature for the TLC and HPLC identification of hypericin (Dorosiev 1985; Ollivier et al 1985; Pachaly 1984; Freytag 1984; Vanhaelen & Vanhaelen-Fastre 1983; Chialva et al 1983; Steinbach 1981; Katalin et al 1981). Katalin et al (1982) report on the histological examination of St. John's wort leaves. See the *American Herbal Pharmacopoeia* review (Upton 1997) for further details on quality, identification, and standardization methods.

Preparations

The three most effective solvents for hypericin appear to be olive oil, ethanol, and methanol. Methanol is the most efficient solvent and it is inexpensive, which is why most European manufacturers of powdered extracts use it. Ethanol is less effective but still satisfactory. Ethanol and glycerine are only solvents used to make liquid extracts or tinctures.

In oil-based products for external use, hypericin is less important than in products for internal use. Less hypericin is extracted in oil than in ethanol or methanol (Maisenbacher & Kovar 1992). Other compounds such as the flavonoids queretin and biapigenin plus four more, all xanthones, and especially the acylphloroglucides hyperforin and adhyperforin, are also extracted by oil. The hyperforins are widely considered to be the most important active compounds for wound-healing and preventing infections with external application.

Stability. Researchers who studied the stability of the hyperforins in oily commercial products found that half of the samples tested contained significant amounts of the compounds, but after the bottles were opened, they broke down to undetectable levels within five weeks. Commercial products might be more stable if they are stored in the refrigerator, but preventing exposure to air is probably the most important factor for increasing the shelf-life of any St. John's wort product. The hyperforins in a freshly made olive-oil-based St. John's wort product lasted up to three months (Maisenbacher & Kovar 1992). The researchers detected a number of breakdown products with hyperforin-like electron ultraviolet spectra. It is possible that these compounds are also active.

The flavonoid content of St. John's wort oil was three to four times higher when the macerating preparation was exposed to sunlight. The flavonoids probably contribute to the anti-inflammatory effects of oil-based St. John's wort preparations.

Hypericin has been shown to be more effectively extracted with glycol and sunflower seed oil when the moisture content of the herb was between fifty and seventy percent, and two to seven times higher at 70 degrees C. than at 20 degrees C. The menstruum was saturated after twelve hours and twenty-four hours respectively, but it took three to four extractions to exhaust the herb (Georgiev et al 1983). The total extraction in one hour of hypericin with ethanol was not dependent on water content of the herb.

The authors conclude that ethanol is the most suited menstruum for the extraction of dried material (Georgiev et al 1983), although others prefer methanol. Freshly air-dried herb was moistened to seventy to seventy-two percent moisture and extracted at 70 degrees at 1:7 with sunflower seed oil. The total content of hypericin was 2.5 percent, and extraction with ethanol could increase the content to 3.32 percent (a 25-percent increase) (Georgiev et al 1983).

Ed Smith of Herb Pharm has extracted the fresh flowering tops and compared them to the freshly dried extract of the plant using high-performance thin-layer chromatography (HPTLC). He found higher hypericin levels in the dried-plant extract (Smith 1997). This seems to indicate that the best way to make a potent tincture is to powder the freshly dried herb (up to one month after drying) and macerate in seventy-five percent ethanol for two weeks, shaking vigorously for a few minutes daily.

Hypericin content of commercial products is reasonably stable, but exposure to heat and direct sunlight will speed their breakdown. Hypericin in a juice of *H. perforatum* and a powdered extract dropped by 14 percent during one year, and the dry extract remained stable when stored at 20 degrees C. When stored at 60 degrees C, the hypericin content dropped 33 percent in powdered extract, 33 percent in tablets, and 47 percent in liquid juice (Adamski & Styp-Rekowska 1971).

In one extensive study, up to eighty percent of the hypericin was destroyed by drying the fresh plant in sunlight (Araya & Ford 1981). For this reason, modern herbalists generally grind the fresh tops of *Hypericum* and immediately macerate them in olive oil or sunflower-seed oil, or as Smith determined, the freshly shade-dried top five inches of the flowering plant. The oil is then pressed and filtered after two weeks and should be stored in amber bottles away from heat and light. An alcoholic tincture is made in the same way, macerating the fresh, ground tops in seventy to ninety percent ethyl alcohol and up to thirty percent distilled water. St. John's wort is currently official in the pharmacopoeias of Czechoslovakia, Poland, Romania, and the Soviet Union (Reynolds 1993).

THE ENERGETICS OF *HYPERICUM* IN TRADITIONAL MEDICINE

In herbal medicine, herbalists consider the nature of a healing plant as important as its uses. Herbs have "energetic" properties, such as hot, cold, dry, and moist, that determine exactly how they should be used and by what kind of person. In the early humoral system of medicine, Galen, a renowned ancient physician, considered *Hypericum*

HISTORIC TREATMENTS OF DEPRESSION

Depression is an age-old affliction. It was noted in Sumaria in the third century B.C., and Egyptian, Minoan, and Greek writers remarked upon the illness as well. Throughout history, cultures have been challenged to find ways of dealing with the suffering and disruption of depression.

Some cultures preferred the opium poppy as a weapon against depression. The Sumerians, Minoans, Egyptians, and many later cultures knew and remarked upon it as a remedy for what we now call depression.

Fermented drinks containing the drug ethyl alcohol predate written records.

Although alcohol is a depressant, its initial effects of relaxation and relief from worries are very attractive to depressed people. From ancient times until today, depressed people have self-medicated with alcohol or other drugs, sometimes to the point of addiction, and then suffered even deeper depression as the alcohol reveals its true nature.

Other popular mood enhancers of the ancients include belladonna, the deadly nightshade, which has a calming and nervous-system enhancing effect, and henbane and mandrake root, which contain the same active ingredient, the alkaloid atropine. Hashish, marijuana, datura (in the New World), and the *soma* of the Hindus were also important as mood-enhancing substances.

The ancient Greeks and Romans understood and promoted the beneficial effects of music, painting, acting and plays, and dance on the mood of sufferers of depression. Coupled with physiotherapy like hot baths, massage, exercise, and gymnastics, these humane and enlightened therapies formed a rational basis of treatment for many people with mood disorders.

Through the Middle Ages, many who suffered from these illnesses were thrown into "madhouses," cruel and degrading warehouses for the ill. Others were ostracized or killed.

Specific treatment of depression began in the 1950s. The first tricyclic antidepressant, imipramine, was introduced into psychiatry in 1957 and followed by the monoamine oxidase inhibitors (MAOIs). These drugs marked a great advance in treating depression, for they altered the chemistry of the brain itself, a result of growing understanding of the role of serotonin in depression, anxiety, insomnia, and other mood disorders. As this understanding became more complete, drugs advanced accordingly; the selective serotonin reuptake inhibitors (SSRIs) such as Prozac, Paxil, and Zoloft were created. This class of drugs has profoundly positive effects in some individuals, while their side effects were fewer than experienced with previous antidepressants.

Some researchers and physicians are currently saying that St. John's wort might be the next wave of antidepressants. The herb is as effective as pharmaceutical drugs for many kinds of depression and mood disorders, with many fewer side effects.

to be hot and dry. The herbalist Culpeper said that it was under the influence of Leo and the sun.

Modern herbalists, including myself, know that the plant has strong anti-inflammatory properties and thus might say that it has cooling properties. Other modern actions of the herb include antiviral, antidepressive, anodyne (pain-relieving), and wound-healing abilities. These actions seem to be contradictory to the energetic qualities of the plant. My opinion is that the plant is warm and dry in nature; its taste is astringent and slightly pungent, and it primarily influences the nervous, cardiovascular, and integumentary (skin, hair, nails) systems.

CLINICAL STUDIES

To date, a number of clinical reports and drug monitoring studies including more than 5,000 patients have shown St. John's wort preparations to be effective and safe for the relief of mild to moderate depression (Daniel 1951; Pieschl et al 1989; Maisenbacher & Kuhn 1990; Woelk et al 1993). In addition, at least 23 random, double-blind clinical trials have been performed using a variety of products containing standardized extracts of St. John's wort for the treatment of mild to severe depression. The results were mostly positive, with few side effects reported (Linde et al 1996). Table A-4, at the end of this appendix, summarizes the most important data on many of the studies.

CLINICAL APPLICATIONS

Clearly, the potential scope of clinical application of St. John's wort is extensive. However, if one narrows the focus down to those activities that are most mentioned, such as antibacterial, antiphlogistic,

Table A-3. Clinical Indications for St. John's Wort

Herb Source:

Flowers of Hypericum perforatum, *gathered during the time of blooming; or the dried parts above the ground, as well as their preparations, in effective dosages.*

Clinical Applications:

Internally: *Psychovegetative disturbances, depressive states, fear and/or nervous disturbances. Oily* Hypericum *preparations during dyspeptic disturbances.*

Externally: *Oily* Hypericum *preparations for the treatment of abrasive wounds, myalgia (muscular pain), and first-degree burns.*

Contraindications:

None known.

Side effects:

Photosensitization is possible, especially in fair-skinned people.

Interference with other drugs:

None known.

Dosage schedule:

Average daily dose recommended is 2 to 4 grams of the powdered herb, or 0.2-1.0 g hypericin as a powdered extract.

Method of use:

Cut or powdered plant, liquid and solid forms for oral administration. Liquid and semi-solid forms for external use.

Effects:

Mild antidepressant action (monoamineoxidase [MAO] inhibitor), oily preparations have antiphlogistic activity. Diuretic activity, direct effect on smooth musculature.

diuretic, and antidepressive, specific clinical applications become more restricted.

In modern European medicine, St. John's wort extracts are included in many over-the-counter and prescription drugs for mild depression and have clinical application for bedwetting and nightmares in children. The extract is included in diuretic preparations, and the oil is taken internally by the teaspoon to help heal gastritis, gastric ulcers, and inflammatory conditions of the colon (using a retention enema) (Weiss 1988). The oil is also used externally in burn and wound remedies.

Table A-3, taken from the German Health Department's official monograph on St. John's wort (Kommission E, 1984), summarizes the current clinical applications of the plant (Proserpio 1976).

Commission E is a diverse group of pharmacologists, chemists, manufacturers, and practitioners. They were convened and charged by the German government to bring together the available literature on medicinal plants commonly sold in Europe for the purpose of determining their safety, efficacy, and proper dose. Manufacturers are allowed to make claims based on the information in the monographs. Some herbs received a "negative monograph," which means they should not be sold as health products in Germany. The complete Commission E monographs are soon to be published by the American Botanical Council.

This technical review is updated from the original Herbalgram *review.*

Table A-4. Summary of Controlled Studies of
St. John's Wort for Depression and Related Conditions

Condition	Duration	Number of Patients	Type of Study
Mild to moderate depression	4 to 8 weeks	1,757	Meta-analysis of 23 randomized trials; 20 double-blind, 1 single blind, and 2 open label
Depression	—	97	Multicenter, placebo-controlled double-blind trial
Depression	4 weeks	102	Randomized double blind study
Depressive and psychovegetative irritations	4 weeks	40	Randomized, placebo-controlled double-blind study
Sleep quality of older volunteers	4 weeks	12	Double-blind, placebo-controlled cross-over design
Healthy volunteers	4 weeks	24	Random double-blind study

Dosage	Results & Conclusions	References
Varied	Hypericum proved significantly superior to placebo in treating some depressive disorders. Appeared comparably effective to standard antidepressants with fewer side effects.	Linde, 1996
100 to 120 mg twice daily in 70% of the patients (n = 43) equivalent to pharmaceutical.	Significant improvement of depression antidepressants. Reduced anxiety noted.	Witte et al 1995
900 mg of Hypericum extract vs. 75 mg maprotiline	Total score on tests measuring degree of depression dropped by 50% in both groups; similar results in D-S and CGI scale	Harrer et al., 1994.
Hypericum extract LI 160 at 900 mg daily	Assessments done at 0, 2, and 4 weeks showed global significant improvement in treated group, with 70% being free of symptoms after 4 weeks. Lack of activity, tiredness, and disturbed sleep improved greatly.	Hübner, 1994
300 mg hydromethanolic preparation 3 x daily;	Improved sleep quality with increased deep sleep	Schulz & Jobert, 1993.
300 mg hydromethanolic preparation 3 x daily vs. maprotiline, 10 mg 3 x daily	In resting EEG, theta frequencies increased with St. John's wort and decreased with maprotiline (similar changes in alpha and beta frequencies. Results interpreted as improvement of cognitive functions with St. John's wort.	Johnson et al 1993.

Condition	Duration	Number of Patients	Type of Study
Seasonal affective disorder volunteers		20	Single-blind randomized study
Depressive patients	4 weeks	50	Placebo-controlled double-blind
Depressive patients	6 weeks	135	Double-blind
Neurotic depressions or depressive irritations	4 weeks	105	Double-blind, placebo-controlled
Healthy volunteers	6 weeks	12	Double-blind, placebo-controlled crossover with two weeks of medication-free time between the two phases.
Volunteers	8 days	40	Double-blind placebo-controlled
Depressive symptoms	4 weeks	40	Randomized Double-blind study

Dosage	Results & Conclusions	References
0.3% total hypericin in hydromethanolic extract	Antidepressant effect enhanced by light therapy; maximum plasma concentrations 4-6 hours; plasma half-life 24.8-26.5 hours [hypericin] maximum plasma concentrations 2-4 hours; plasma half-life 16.3–36 hours [pseudohypericin].	Martinez et al 1994; Staffeldt et al., 1994
—	Measures of capacity of mental performance were conducted before and during therapy. Results showed significant improvement of cognitive performance during Hypericum extract administration.	Lehr et al 1993
900 mg Hypericum extract vs. 75 mg imipramine	Groups showed parallel reduction of in symptoms of depression. The Hypericum group had fewer and milder side effects.	Vorbach et al 1993
900 mg Hypericum extract	Treatment assessed at 2 & 4 weeks. In the treated group 67% responded.	Harrer and Sommer 1993.
900 mg hydro-methanolic extract	Reduction in alpha, increase in theta and beta frequencies; reduction of audio-visual latencies in evoked potentials was seen	Johnson, 1991
Up to 1 mg daily total hypericin	Photosensitivity was not induced EEG results interpreted as predominantly	Wienert et al, 1991. Kugler et al 1990
0.5 mg total hypericin or 1.4 g	relaxing effect (increase in theta-activity, decrease in alpha-activity)	

REFERENCES

Adamski, R. and E. Styp-Rekowska. 1971. Stability of hypericin in juice, dry extract, and tablets from *Hypericum perforatum* plants. *Farmacja Polska*. 27:237–41.

Aizenman, B.E. 1969. Antibiotic preparations from *Hypericum perforatum*. *Mikrobiologicheskii Zhurnal (Kiev)*. 31:128–33.

Alleyne, J. 1733. *A New English Dispensatory*. London: Thomas Astley.

American Medical Association. 1983. *AMA Drug Evaluations*. Chicago: AMA.

Andersen, D.O. 1991. *In vitro* virucidal activity of selected anthraquinones and anthraquinone derivatives. *Antiviral Res*. 16: 185–96.

Araya, O.S. and E.J.H. Ford. 1981. An investigation of the type of photosensitization caused by the ingestion of St. John's wort *(Hypericum perforatum)* by calves. *Journal of Comparative Pathology*. 91:135–41.

Azaryan, R.A. 1985. Standardization of [quality indexes for the medicinal] herb *Hypericum perforatum*. *Farmatsiya*. 34:18–21.

Bailey, L.H. 1930. *The Standard Cyclopedia of Horticulture*. London: Macmillan Co.

Barnard, D.L. et al. 1992. Evaluation of the antiviral activity of anthraquinones, anthrones and anthraquinone derivatives against human cytomegalovirus. *Antiviral Res*. 17: 63–77.

Baureithel, K.H. et al. 1997. Inhibition of benzodiazepine binding in vitro by amentoflavone, a constituent of various species of Hypericum. Pharmaceutica Acta Helvetiae 72(3):153–7.

Barton, B.H. and T. Castle. 1877. *The British Flora Medica: A History of the Medicinal Plants of Great Britain*. London: Chatto and Windus.

Bensky, D. and A. Gamble. 1993. *Chinese Herbal Medicine*

Materia Medica. Seattle: Eastland Press.

Berghoefer, R. and J. Hoelzl. 1987. Bioflavonoids in *Hypericum perforatum.* Part 1. Isolation of 13, II8-biapigenin. *Planta Medica.* 53:216–17.

Berkow, R. ed. 1982. *The Merck Manual.* Rahway, NJ: Merck Research Laboratories.

Bladt, S. and H. Wagner. 1993. MAO-Hemmung durch Fraktionen und Inhaltsstoffe von *Hypericum*-Extrakt. *Nervenheilkunde* 12:349–52.

Bladt, S. and H. Wagner. 1994. Inhibition of MAO by fractions and constituents of *Hypericum* extract. *Journal of Geriatric Psychiatry and Neurology.* 7:S57–59.

Blumenthal, M. et al. (Work in progress). *Commission E Herbal Monographs.*

Boericke, W. 1927. *Materia Medica with Repertory.* Philadelphia: Boericke and Runyon.

Bol'shakova, I.V. 1997. Antioxidant properties of a series of extracts from medicinal plants. *Biofizika.* 42(2):480–3.

Bombardelli, E. and P. Morazzoni. 1995. *Hypericum perforatum. Fitoterapia.* 66:43–68.

Bramtmer, A. et al. 1994. Untersuchungen zur antiphlogistischen Wirkung von *Hypericum perforatum* L. *Sci Pharm.* 62:97–8.

Brockmann, H. et al. 1974. Zur isolierung und konstitution des pseudohypericins. *Tetrahedron Letters.* 23:1991–94.

Brondz, I. and T. Greibrokk. 1983. N-1-alkanols of *Hypericum Perforatum. Journal of Natural Products.* 46:940–41.

Cada, D. et al. 1997. *Drug Facts and Comparisons.* St. Louis: Facts and Comparisons.

Campbell, M. H. et al. 1979. Effect of time of application of herbicides on the long-term control of St. John's wort *(Hypericum perforatum* var. *angustifolium). Australian Journal of Experimental Agriculture and Animal Husbandry.* 101:746–48.

Chialva, F. et al. 1981. Study on the composition of the

essential oil from *Hypericum perforatum* L. and *Teucrium chamaedrys* L. *Rivista Italiana EPPOS.* 63:286–88.

Chialva, F. et al. 1983. Direct headspace gas chromatographic analysis with glass capillary columns in quality control of aromatic herbs. *Journal of Chromatography.* 279:333–40.

Clare, N.T. 1952. Photosensitization in diseases of domestic animals. *Review Series No. 3 of the Commonwealth Bureau of Animal Health.* Bucks, England: Commonwealth Agricultural Bureau.

Costes, C. and T. Chantal. 1967. Carotenoid pigments of the petals of the inflorescence of St. John's wort *(Hypericum perforatum). Annals of Physiology.* Veg. 9:157–77.

Culpeper, N. 1847. *The Complete Herbal.* London: Thomas Kelly.

Curle, P. et al. 1988. Neurochemical studies on *Valeriana* and *Hypericum.* Battelle-Europe Report Nr. 2107, unpublished (from ESCOP, 1996).

Daniel, K. 1951. Kurze Mitteilung über 12 jährige therapeutische Erfahrungen mit Hypericin. *Klin. Wschr.* 29: 260–62.

Degar, S. et al. 1993. Photodynamic inactivation of radiation leukemia virus produced from hypericin-treated cells. *Virology.* 197:796–800.

Deihl, J.R. 1932. Kava and kava-drinking. *Primitive Man.* 5(4). 61–68.

Demisch, L. et al. 1989. Identification of selective MAO-type-A inhibitors in *Hypericum perforatum* L. (Hyperforat). *Pharmacopsychiat* 22: 194.

Demisch, L. et al. 1991. *Einfluß einer subchronischen Gabe von Hyperforat auf die nächtliche Melatonin- und Kortisolsekretion bei Probanden (abstract).* Nürnberg: AGNP-Symposium.

Derbentseva, N.A. and A.S. Rabinovich. 1968. Isolation, purification, and study of some physicochemical properties of novoimanin in *Novoimanin Ego Lech Svoistva.* 15–18.

Derbentseva, N.A. et al. 1972. Effect of tannins from *Hyper-*

icum perforatum on influenza viruses. *Mikrobiologicheskii Zhurnal (Kiev).* 34:768–72.

DeSmet, P.A. and W.A. Nolen. 1996. St. John's wort as an antidepressant. *British Medical Journal.* 313:241–47.

Dittmann, J. et al. 1971. Normalizing glucose metabolism in brain tumor slices by hyperoside. *Arzneimittel-Forschung.* 21:1999–2002.

Dorosiev, I. 1985. Determination of flavonoids in *Hypericum perforatum. Pharmazie.* 40:585–86.

Ernst, E. 1995. St. John's wort, an anti-depressant? A systematic, criteria-based review. *Phytomedicine.* 2:47–71.

ESCOP. 1996. *Monograph: St. John's wort.* European Scientific Cooperative for Phytomedicines.

Evstifeeva, T.A. and S.V. Sibiriak. 1996. The immunotropic properties of biologically active products obtained from Klamath weed *(Hypericum perforatum* L.). *Eksperimentalnaia i Klinicheskaia Farmakologiia.* 59(1):51–4.

FDA. 1980. Unsafe herbs. *FDA Compliance Policy Guideline* 7117.04.

Federal Register. 1967. Title 221, part 121, subpart D (121:1163). 32:79. Sept. 15.

Felter, H.W. and J.U. Lloyd. 1985. (1898). *King's American Dispensatory* (18th edition). Portland: Eclectic Medical Publications.

Fernie, W.T. 1897. *Herbal Simples.* Bristol: John Wright and Co.

Freytag, W.E. 1984. Determination of hypericin and pseudo-hypericin in *Hypericum perforatum* L. with HPLC. *Deutsche Apotheker-Zeitung.* 124:2383–85.

Garrett, B.J. et al. 1982. Consumption of poisonous plants *(Senecio jacobaea, Symphytum officinale, Pteridium aquilinum, Hypericum perforatum)* by rats: Chronic toxicity, mineral metabolism, and hepatic drug-metabolizing enzymes. *Toxicology Letters.* 10:183–88.

Georgiev, E. et al. 1983. Effect of solvent and moisture of St. John's wort on extraction of

some biologically active substances. II. Extraction of hypericin with glycol. Nauchni
Tr.–Vissh Inst. Khranit.
Vkusova Prom-st. *Plovdiv.*
32:251–56.

Gerard, J. 1975. (1633). *The
Herbal.* New York: Dover
Publications.

Gonsette, R.E. 1982. Treatment of multiple sclerosis.
*Bulletin de la Societe Belge
d'Ophtamologie.* 199–200;
271–80.

Gozin, A.A. and V.S. Yasnetsov.
1979. Effect of mineral fertil-
izers on the content levels of
biologically active substances
in common St. John's wort.
Dep. Doc., VINITI 2208–79.

Greene, T. 1824. *The Universal
Herbal.* London: Caxton
Press.

Griffith, R.E. 1847. *Medical
Botany.* Philadelphia: Lea and
Blanchard.

Gunther, R.T. 1933. *The Greek
Herbal of Dioscorides.*:Hafner
Publishing Co.

Gurevich, A.I. et al. 1971. Hyperforin, an antibiotic from

*Hypericum perforatum. Antibi-
otiki.* 16:510–12.

Hänsgen, K.D. et al. 1994. Mul-
ticenter double-blind study
examining the antidepressant
effectiveness of the *Hypericum*
extracts LI 160. *Nerven-
heilkunde.* 12:185–89.

Harrer, G. et al. 1994. Effectiveness and tolerance of the
Hypericum extract LI 1 60 in
comparison with imipramine:
Randomized double-blind
study with 135 outpatients.
*Journal of Geriatric Psychiatry
and Neurology.* 7:S24–28.

Hickey, M. and C. King. 1981.
*100 Families of Flowering
Plants.* Cambridge: Cam-
bridge University Press.

Hill, J. 1808. *The Family Herbal.*
Bungay: Brightly and T. Kin-
nersley.

Hobbs, C. 1989 St. John's Wort:
A Review. *HerbalGram.* 18/19:
24–33.

Hobbs, C. 1996. *The Ginsengs, A
User's Guide.* Santa Cruz, CA:
Botanica Press.

Hobbs, C. 1997. *Stress and Natural Healing.* Santa Cruz, CA:

Botanica Press/Interweave Press.

Hölzl, J. and E. Ostrowski. 1987. St John's wort *(Hypericum perforatum* L.) HPLC analysis of the main components and their variability in a population. *Deutsche Apotheker-Zeitung.* 127:1227–30.

Hölzl, J. 1989. Johanniskraut— eine alte Arzneipflanze mit neuer Bedeutung. *Therapeutikon.* 3:540–7.

Hölzl, J. 1993. Inhaltstoffe und Wirkmechanismen des Johanniskrautes. *Z. Phytother.* 14:255–64.

Hohnen Oil Co., Ltd. 1985. Encapsulated health food supplements. Japanese patent: JP 85149637A2, date: 850806.

Holtje, H.D. and A. Walper. 1993. Molecular modeling of the antidepressive mechanism of *Hypericum* ingredients. *Nervenheilkunde.* 12:339–40.

Hübner, W.D. et al. 1994. *Hypericum* treatment of mild depression with somatic symptoms. *Journal of Geriatric Psychiatry and Neurology.* 7:S12–14.

Hudson, J.B. et al. 1994. Antiviral activities of hypericin. *Antiviral Research.* 15:101–12.

Jaeger, E.C. 1972. *A Source-Book of Biological Names and Terms.* Springfield, IL: Charles C. Thomas.

James, J.S. 1992. Hypericin. *AIDS Treatment News.* Feb. 1992, 146: 1–4.

James, L.F. and A.E. Johnson. 1976. Some major plant toxicities of the western United States. *Journal of Range Management.* 29–356–63.

Johnson, D. 1991. Neurophysiologische Wirkungen von *Hypericum* im Doppelblindversuch mit Probanden. *Nervenheilkunde* 12: 328–30.

Johnson, D. et al. 1993. Wirkungen von Johanniskraut-Extrakt LI 160 im Vergleich mit Maprotilin auf Ruhe-EEG und evozierte Potentiale bei 24 Probanden. *Nervenheilkunde* 12: 328–30.

Jones, W.H.S. 1964. *Pliny— Natural History.* Cambridge: Harvard University Press.

Karryev, M.O. and N.F. Komissarenko. 1980. Phytochemical study of *Hypericum* L. Plants of the Turkmenian flora. *Izvestiya Akademii Nauk Turkmenskoi SSR, Seriya Biologicheskikh Nauk.* 52–57

Kartnig, T. et al. 1996. Production of hypericin, pseudohypericin, and flavonoids in cell cultures of various *Hypericum* species and their chemotypes. *Planta Med.* 62(1):51–3.

Kasper, S. et al. 1996. *Hypericum* in the treatment of seasonal affective disorders. *2nd International Congress on Phytomedicine.* Munich.

Katalin, I. et al. 1982. Ultrastructural examination of leaf differentiation in St. John's wort. *Herba Hungarica.* 21:21–37.

Khosa, R.L. and N. Bhatia. 1982. Antifungal effect of *Hypericum perforatum. Journal of Scientific Research of Plants and Medicines.* 3:49–50.

King, John. 1876. *The American Dispensatory.* Cincinnati: Wilstach, Baldwin and Co.

Kitanov, G. 1983. Determination of the absolute configuration of catechins isolated from *Hypericum perforatum. Farmatsiya.* 33:19–22.

Kitanov, G.M. and K.F. Blinova. 1987. Modern state of the chemical study of species of the genus *Hypericum. Chemistry of Natural Compounds.* 23:151–66.

Koget, T.A. 1972. Determination of the amount of quercitin in *Hypericum perforatum. Khimiya Prirodnykh Soedinenii.* 2:242–43.

Kraus, G.A. et al. 1990. Antiretroviral activity of synthetic hypericin and related analogs. *Biochem. Biophys. Res. Commun.* 172: 149–53.

Lavie, G. et al. 1989. Studies of the mechanisms of action of the antiretroviral agents hypericin and pseudohypericin. *Proceedings of the National Academy of Science.* 86:5963–67.

Leathwood, P.D. and F. Chauffard. 1985. Aqueous extract of

valerian reduces sleep latency to fall asleep in man. *Planta Medica.* 51:144–48.

Lehman, E. et al. 1996. Efficacy of a special kava extract *(Piper methysticum)* in patients with states of anxiety, tension and excitedness of non-mental origin: A double-blind placebo-controlled study of four weeks' treatment. *Phytomedicine.* III(2). 113–19.

Lenard, J. et al. 1993. Photodynamic inactivation of infectivity of human immunodeficiency virus and other enveloped viruses using hypericin and rose bengal: Inhibition of fusion and syncytia formation. *Proceedings of the National Academy of Science.* 90:158–62.

Leung, A. and S. Foster. 1996. *Encyclopedia of Common Natural Ingredients.* New York: John Wiley and Sons.

Linde, K. et al. 1996. St. John's wort for depression: An overview and meta-analysis of randomized clinical trials. *British Medical Journal.* 313:253–58.

Lindley, J. 1838. *Flora Medica.* London: Longman, Orme, Brown, Green and Longmans.

Lopez-Bazzocchi, I. et al. 1991. Antiviral Activity of the Photoactive Plant Pigment Hypericin. *Photochemistry and Photobiology.* 54:95–98.

Lust, J. 1974. *The Herb Book.* New York: Bantam Publishing.

Madaus, G. 1938. *Handbook of Biological Medicine* (3 vols.) (reprint). New York: Georg Olms Verlag.

Madaus, G. 1938. *Lehrbuch der Biologischen Heilmittel.* Leipsig, Germany: Georg Thieme.

Maisenbacher, H.J. and U. Kuhn. 1990. Therapie von Depressionen in der Praxis. Ergebnisse einer Anwendungsbeobachtung mit Hyperici herbs. *Natura Med.* 7:394–99.

Maisenbacher, P. and K.-A. Kovar. 1992. Analysis and stability of Hyperici Oleum. *Planta Medica.* 58: 351–54.

Maksyutina, N.P. and T.A. Koet. 1971. Polyphenols from the

grass *Hypericum perforatum* and the preparation novoimanin. *Khimiya Prirodnykh Soedinenii.* 7:363–67.

Marsh, C.D. 1930. Toxic effect of St. John's wort *(Hypericum perforatum)* on cattle and sheep. *USDA Technical Bulletin*, No. 202.

Martinez, B. et al. 1994. *Hypericum* in the treatment of seasonal affective disorders. *Journal of Geriatric Psychiatry and Neurology.* 7:S29–33.

Mathis, C. and G. Ourisson. 1963. Etude chimio-taxonomique du genre Hypericum. *Phytochemistry.* 2:157–71.

Mathis, C. and G. Ourisson. 1964. Etude chimio-taxonomique du genre *Hypericum*-III. *Phytochemistry.* 3:133–41.

McGuffin, M. et al. 1997. *The Botanical Safety Handbook.* Boca Raton: CRC Press.

Merck and Co. 1907. *Merck's 1907 Index.* St. Louis: Merck and Co.

Meruelo, D. et al. 1988. Therapeutic agents with dramatic

antiretroviral activity and little toxicity at effective doses: Aromatic polycyclic diones hypericin and pseudohypericin. *Proceedings of the National Academy of Science.* 85:5230–34.

Moerman, D.E. 1986. *Medicinal Plants of Native America.* Ann Arbor: University of Michigan Museum of Anthropology.

Moore, M. 1979. *Medicinal Plants of the Mountain West.* Santa Fe: Museum of New Mexico Press.

Morelli, I. et al. 1983. Selected medicinal plants. FAO Plant Production and Protection Paper 53/1, Rome.

Mori, M. 1982. N-hexacosanol and n-octacosanol: Feeding stimulants on the larvae of the silkworm, *Bombyx mori. Journal of Insect Physiology.* 28:969–73.

Müldner, H. and M. Zöller. 1984. Antidepressive Wirkung eines auf den Wirkstoffkomplex Hypericin standardisierten *Hypericum*-Extraktes. Biochemische und klinische Untersuchungen. *Arzniem-Forsch.*/Drug Res. 34: 918–20.

Müller, W.E.G. and R. Rossol.
1993. Einfluß von *Hypericum*-
Extrakt auf die Expression
von Serotonin-Rezeptoren.
Nervenheilkunde. 12: 357–58.

Müller, W.E. and R. Rossel.
1994. Effects of *Hypericum*
extract on the suppression of
serotonin receptors. *Journal
of Geriatric Psychiatry and
Neurology.* 7:S63–64.

National Academy of Sciences.
1975. *Herbal Pharmacology in
the People's Republic of China.*
Washington, D.C.: NAS.

Negrash, A.K. and P. Y. Pochinok. 1972. Comparative
study of chemotherapeutic
and pharmacological properties of antimicrobial preparations from common St.
John's wort. *Fitonotsidy.
Mater. Soveshch.* 6th. Meet-
ing,1969. 198–200.

Nielsen, M. and P. Arends.
1978. Structure of Xanthono-
lignoid Dielcorin. *Phytochemistry.* 17:2040.

Nielsen, M. et al. 1988. High
affinity of the naturally occur-
ing biflavonoid, amento-
flavon, to brain benzodi-
azepine receptors in vitro.

Biochem. Pharmacol. 37:
3285–87.

Nordfors, M. and P. Hartvig.
1997. St. John's wort against
depression in favour again.
Lakartidningen. 94(25):
2365–7.

Noris, F.H. et al. 1986. Trial of
octacosanol in amyotrophic
lateral sclerosis: Part I. *Neurology.* (USA) 36/9:1263–64.

Okpanyi, S.N. and M.L. Weis-
cher. 1987. Experimental animal studies of the psychotropic activity of a *Hypericum*
extract. *Arzneimittel-
Forschung.* 37:10–13.

Ollivier, B. et al. 1985. Separa-
tion and identification of phe-
nolic acids by high-performance chromatography and
ultraviolet spectorscopy. Application to *Parietaria offici-
nalis* L. and to St. John's wort
(*Hypericum perforatum* L.).
*Journal de Pharmacie de Bel-
gique.* 40:173–77.

Osol, A. and G.E. Farrar, Jr.
1955. *The Dispensatory of the
United States of America* (25th
ed.). Philadelphia: Lippincott
Co.

Pace, N. and G. MacKinney. 1941. Hypericin, the photo-dynamic pigment from St. John's wort. *Journal of the American Chemistry Society.* 63:2570–74.

Pachaly, P. 1984. Thin-layer chromatography in the pharmacy: Practical examples. *Deutsche Apotheker-Zeitung.* 124:2153–61.

Pennington, J.A.T. (Ed.) 1994. *Bowes and Church's Food Values of Portions Commonly Used* (16th ed.). Philadelphia: J.P. Lippincott Company.

Perovic, S. and W.E. Muller. 1995. Pharmacological profile of *Hypericum* extract. Effect on serotonin uptake by post-synaptic receptors. *Arzneimittel-Forschung*, 1995 Nov, 45(11):1145–8.

Pickering, C. 1879. *Chronological History of Plants.* Boston: Little, Brown and Co.

Pieschl, D. et al. 1989. Zur Behandlung von Depressionen. Verbundstudie mit einem pflanzlichen Extrakt aus Johanniskraut. *Therapiewoche.* 39: 2567–71.

Pratt, A. 1898. *The Flowering Plants, Grasses, Sedges, and Ferns of Great Britain.* London: Frederick Warne and Co.

Prokosheva, L.I. and L.V. Shatunova. 1985. Content of active substances in the aboveground parts of *Hypericum perforatum. Rastitel'nye Resursy.* 21:461:63.

Proserpio, G. 1976. Natural sunscreens: Vegetable derivatives as sunscreens and tanning agents. *Cosmetic Toiletries.* 91:34, 39–44.

Rakel, R.E. (Ed.). 1996. *Conn's Current Therapy.* Philadelphia: W.B. Saunders.

Reynolds, J.E.F. (ed.). 1993. *Martindale, The Extra Pharmacopeia.* London: The Pharmaceutical Press.

Robson, N. K. B. 1978. Flora of Panama, 6, family 123A Hypericaceae. *Annals of the Missouri Botanical Garden.* 65:9–26.

Roth, L. et al. 1984. *GiftpflanzenùPflanzengifte.* Munich: Ecomed.

Saljic, J. 1975. Ointment for the treatment of burns. *German Offenlegungschrift.* 2,406,452 (CL. A61K). 21 August.

Sargent, M. 1994. http://www.nimh.nih.gov/pub licat/ptdep.htm

Schinazi, R.F. et al. 1990. Anthraquinones as a new class of antiviral agents against human immunodeficiency virus. *Antiviral Res.* 265–72.

Schleel, L.D. 1972. Photosensitizing agents. In *Toxicants Occurring Naturally in Food.* Washington, D.C.: National Academy of Sciences.

Schulz, H. and M. Jobert. 1993. Der Einfluß von Johanniskraut-Extrakt auf das Schiaf-EEG bei älteren Probandinnen. *Nervenheilkunde.* 12:323–27.

Shakirova, K.K. et al. 1970. Antimicrobial properties of some species of St. John's wort cultivated in Uzbekistan. *Mikrobiologicheskii Zhurnal (Kiev).* 32:494–97.

Smith, E. 1997. Personal communication.

Snider, S.R. 1984. Octacosanol in Parkinsonism [letter]. *Annals of Neurology.* 16:723.

Sommer, H. and G. Harrer. 1994. Placebo-controlled double-blind study examining the effectiveness of a *Hypericum* preparation in 105 mildly depressed patients. *Journal of Geriatric Psychiatry and Neurology.* 7:S9–11.

Sparenberg, B. et al. 1993. Untersuchungen über antidepressive Wirkstoffe von Johanniskraut. *Pharm. Ztg. Wiss.* 138:50–4.

Staffeldt, B. et al. 1994. Pharmacokinetics of hypericin and pseudohypericin after oral intake of the *Hypericum perforatum* extract LI 160 in healthy volunteers. State Historical Society of Wisconsin. 1944. *Pharmacopoeia Londinensis of 1618.* Reproduced in facsimile. Madison: State Historical Society.

Steinbach, R.A. 1981. Problems in the purification and standardization of plant drugs, for example, *Hypericum. Zeitschrift fuer Angewandte Phytotherapie.* 2:224–24.

Steinbeck-Klose, A. P. Wernet. 1993. Successful long term te=reatment over 40 months of HIV-patients with intravenous Hypericin. International Conference on AIDS. Abstract PO.B.26-2012.

Sticher, O. 1977. Plant mono-, di- and sesquiterpenoids with pharmacological or therapeutical activity. In *New Natural Products and Plant Drugs with Pharmacological, Biological or Therapeutical Activity.* H. Wagner and P. Wolff, Eds. New York: Springer-Verlag.

Stoyanova, A. et al. 1987. Thin-layer chromatography of extracts of *Hypericum perforatum. Farmatsiya.* 1:8–13.

Suzuki, O. et al. 1980. Inhibition of type A and type B monoamine oxidase by isogentisin and its 3–0-glucoside. *Planta Medica.* 42:17–21.

Suzuki, O. et al. 1984. Inhibition of monoamine oxidase by hypericin. *Planta Medica.* 50:272–74.

Takahashi, I. et al. 1989. Hypericin and pseudohypericin specifically inhiit protein kinase C: Possible relation to their antiretroviral activity. *Biochem. Res. Commun.* 165: 1207–12.

Takhtajan, A. I. 1980. Outline of the classification of flowering plants (Magnoliophyta). *Botanical Review.* 46:225.

Tandan, R. and W.G. Bradley. 1985. Amyotrophic lateral sclerosis: Part I. Clinical features, pathology, and ethical issues in management. *Annals of Neurology.* (USA) 18/3:271–80.

Thiede, H.M. & A. Walper. 1993. MAO- und COMT-Hemmung durch *Hypericum*-Extrakte und Hypericin. *Nervenheilkunde* 12: 346–8.

Thiede, H.M. and A. Walper. 1994. Inhibition of MAO and COMT by *Hypericum* extracts and hypericin. *Journal of Geriatric Psychiatry and Neurology.* 7:S54–56.

Thiele, B. et al. 1993. Modulation der Zytokin-Expression durch *Hypericum*-Extrakt. *Nervenheilkunde* 12: 353–56.

Thiele, B. et al. 1994. Modulation of cytokine expression

by *Hypericum* extract. *Journal of Geriatric Psychiatry and Neurology*. 7:S54–56.

Todd, R.G. 1967. *Martindale's Extra Pharmacopoeia*. London: The Pharmaceutical Press.

Upton, R. 1997. St. John's Wort, the American Herbal Pharmacopeia monograph. *HerbalGram*, 40: 1–82

Vander, A.J. et al. 1970. *Human Physiology*. New York: McGraw-Hill Book Co.

Vanhaelen, M. and R. Vanhaelen-Fastre. 1983. Quantitative determination of biologically active constituents in medicinal plant crude extracts by thin-layer chromatography-densitometry. *Journal of Chromatography*. 281:263–71.

Vickery, A.R. 1981. Traditional uses and folklore of *Hypericum* in the British Isles. *Economic Botany*. 35:289–95.

Vogel, V. 1970. *American Indian Medicine*. Norman, OK: University of Oklahoma Press.

Vonsover, A. et al. 1993. HIV-1 virus load in the serum of AIDS patients undergoing long-term therapy with hypericin. International Conference on AIDS. Abstract Mo.B. 1377

Vonsover, A. et al. 1996. HIV-1 virus load in the serum of AIDS patients undergoing long-term therapy with hypericin. International Conference on AIDS, Vancouver, 1996. Mo. B. 1377.

Vorbach, E.U. et al. 1994. Effectiveness and tolerance of the *Hypericum* extract LI 16 0 in comparison with imipramine: Randomized double-blind study with 135 outpatients. *Journal of Geriatric Psychiatry and Neurology*.

Wagner, H. & S. Bladt. 1994. Pharmaceutical Quality of *Hypericum* Extracts. *Journal of Geriatric Psychiatry & Neurology*. 7:S65–S68.

Weer, N.D. 1994. The antiviral agent hypericin has in vitro activity against HSV-1 through non-specific association with viral and cellular membranes. *Antiviral Chemistry & Chemotherapy*. 5:83–90.

Wienert, V. et al. 1992. Zur Frage der Photosensibilisierung von Hypericin in einer Baldrian-Johanniskraut-Kombination—klinisch-experimentelle, palzebokontrollierte Vergleichsstudie [poster abstract]. Lbeck-Travemnde: 3. Phytotherapie-Kongre, 3–6 October 1991; Poster P23.

Weiss, R.F. 1986. *Herbal Medicine.* Gothenburg, Sweden: AB Arcanum.

Werbach, M.R. 1987. *Nutritional Influences on Illness.* Tarzana, CA: Third Line Press.

Wichtl, M. 1986. *Hypericum perforatum* L. Das Johanniskraut. *Zeitschrift fur Phytotherapie.* 3:87–90.

Woelk, H. et al. 1993. Nutzen und Risikobewertung des *Hypericum*-Extraktes LI 160 auf der Basis einer Drug-Monitoring-Studie mit 3250 Patienten. *Nervenheilkunde* 12: 308–13.

Woelk, H. et al. 1994. Benefits and risks of the *Hypericum* extract LI 160: Drug monitoring study with 3250 patients. *Journal of Geriatric Psychiatry and Neurology.*

Yamashita, M. et al. 1986. Aqueous compositions containing octacosanol. Japanese patent: JP 86263937, date: 861121.

Zaichikova, S.G. et al. 1985. Study of the healing properties and determination of the upper parameters of toxicity of Hypericum. *Farmatisiya.* 1:62.

RESOURCE DIRECTORY

MAIL-ORDER SOURCES FOR HERBS AND PRODUCTS

Essential Oils

Oak Valley Herb Farm
PO Box 2482
Nevada City, CA 95959
(Order by mail only)

Original Swiss Aromatics
PO Box 6723
San Rafael, CA 94903
(415) 479-3979

Simplers Botanical Co.
PO Box 39
Forestville, CA 95436
(707)887-2012

Herbal Extracts

Avena Botanicals
219 Mill Street
Rockport, ME 04856
(207) 594-0694

Enzymatic Therapy
825 Challenger Drive
Green Bay, WI 54311
(800) 225-9245

Herbs, Etc.
1340 Rufina Circle
Santa Fe, NM 87505
(800) 634-3727

Herb Pharm
20260 Williams Highway
Williams, OR 97544
(800) 348-4372

McZand Herbals
4063 Redwood Avenue
Los Angeles, CA 90066
(800) 800-0405

Rainbow Light
207 McPherson
Santa Cruz, CA 95060
(800) 635-1233

Herbs in Bulk

Blessed Herbs
109 Barrie Plains Road
Oakham, MA 01068
(800) 489-4372

Frontier Cooperative Herbs
PO Box 299
Norway, IA 52318
(800) 669-3275

Moonrise Herbs
826 G. St.
Arcata, CA 95521
(800) 603-8364

Starwest Botanicals
11253 Trade Center Drive
Rancho Cordova, CA
  95742
(800) 800-4372

Trinity Herbs
2211 Joy Road
Bodega, CA 94922
(707) 824-2040

Dryers

American Harvest
(800) 288-4545

Grain Alcohol

Aaper Alcohol
Box 339
Shelbyville, KY 40065
(800) 626-5281

McCormick Distilling Co.
Weston, MO 64098
(888) 640-4041

Associations for Depression

National Association for the Mentally Ill (NAMI)
2101 Wilson Blvd.
Suite 302
Arlington, VA 22201
(703) 524-7600

Herb Associations

American Botanical Council
6200 Manor Road
Austin, TX 78723
(512) 331-8868

American Herb Products Association
4733 Bethesda Avenue
Bethesda, MD 20814
(301) 951-3204

Herb Research Foundation
1007 Pearl St.
Boulder, CO 80302
(303) 449-2265

Recommended Reading

Chopra, Deepak. 1994. *The Seven Spiritual Laws of Success*. San Rafael, CA: New World Library.

Coelho, Paulo. 1988. *The Alchemist*. San Francisco: Harper.

Kabat-Zinn, Jon. 1994. *No Matter Where You Go, There You Are*. New York: Hyperion.

Weil, Andrew. 1997. *Eight Weeks to Optimum Health*. New York: Random House.

Inspirational Audio Tapes

Nhat-Hanh, Thich. 1996. *The Long Road Turns to Joy: A Guide to Walking Meditation*. Berkeley: Parallax Press.

Nhat-Hanh, Thich. 1991. *Peace is Every Step: The Path of Mindfulness in Everyday Life*. Edited by Arnold Kotler. New York: Bantam.

INDEX